CONFESSIONS OF A RELIGIONLESS CHRISTIAN

Gene Owens

ABINGDON PRESS

NASHVILLE   NEW YORK

CONFESSIONS OF A RELIGIONLESS CHRISTIAN

Copyright © 1975 by Abingdon Press

Library of Congress Cataloging in Publication Data

Owens, Gene, 1930-
    Confessions of a religionless Christian.
    I. Religion. 2. Christianity—Essence, genius, nature.
I. Title.
BR121.2.094   200'.1   75-14317

ISBN 0-687-09386-4

Scripture quotations unless otherwise noted are from the Revised
Standard Version of the Bible, copyrighted 1946, 1952, and 1971 by
the Division of Christian Education, National Council of Churches,
and are used by permission.

Scripture quotation noted NEB is from the New English Bible,
copyright © the Delegates of the Oxford University Press and the
Syndics of the Cambridge University Press, 1961, 1970.

Text on page 15 is from "Choruses from 'The Rock'" in *Collected
Poems* 1909-1962 by T. S. Eliot, copyright, 1936, by Harcourt Brace
Jovanovich, Inc.; copyright, 1963, 1964, by T. S. Eliot. Reprinted by
permission of the publishers, Harcourt Brace Jovanovich, Inc., and
Faber and Faber. Ltd.

Text on pages 37, 47, and 78 is from *Collected Longer Poems* copyright
© 1969 by W. H. Auden, text on pages 41 and 83 is from *Collected
Shorter Poems* copyright © 1966 by W. H. Auden, and text on pages
106-7 is from *City Without Walls and Other Poems* copyright © 1969 by
W. H. Auden, published by Random House, Inc.

MANUFACTURED BY THE PARTHENON PRESS AT
NASHVILLE, TENNESSEE, UNITED STATES OF AMERICA

To Louise and Gus—
the first essential forms I knew

Preface

For ten years I taught pastoral theology generally and preaching specifically in theological schools in Canada, the United States, and Switzerland. For the past six years I have been doing public penance as a parish minister—seeking absolution for what I taught.

The composition of these essays has caused me to realize that my penance has been far too limited. My sin was not only teaching homiletics without having endured the discipline of weekly sermon preparation; I was also guilty of selling my birthright for a mess of "religionless Christianity."

The phrase sounded so healing for my condition and for the condition of church in the world.

Religious forms were barriers separating God from persons; I was certain of it. My gospel-song memory kept repeating the words "Nothing between my soul and the Savior." For years I wanted electricity without wires.

These peripatetic essays are my confessions in *sacramentum*. They are my wrestlings with the forms of faith that dwell beside the river crossings of life. Now I am experiencing the exhilaration of worthy adversaries, and I know something of sacramental blessing that leaves one limping toward the future.

I am grateful to Myers Park Baptist Church which has seconded my struggle, to my family who has hoped for victory and the periodic peace that follows, to Linda Christopher who helped pull and push thoughts into shape, and to Lillian (Scrappy) Gardner who recorded it all.

Contents

I.
Religion: Form or Fever

Once upon a time a wicked witch turned a handsome prince into a frog. The evil spell could be broken only if the frog were kissed by a princess. O the thrill to childish hearts when that conversion occurred! Alas, somewhere in that pond there was a female frog who cried herself to sleep, croaking, "Never fall in love with a form."

Too few children of God ever hear the addendum to this fairy tale; though they might have heard something similar had they not given up their "daily Bible reading" so early in the educational process. It is *dabhar* Yahweh, say the ancient authors: "You shall not make yourself a graven image, or any likeness of anything . . . . you shall not bow down to them or serve them" (Exodus 20:4-5).

It is law, written upon the heart, taught diligently to children, weaving in and out of conversations, last on your mind when you fall asleep, first when you awake. It is law, as clear as the speck on your glasses, posted on the entrance to your house for all to see. It is law in the heart, the gut, the sinews. It is Torah—the law of life in the community of grace.

Torah was never meant to be a stand-in for God. It is pointer, sign, reminder. Torah is the hunger pang calling attention to food, memory reminding us of loved ones and mediating their presence—a *form* of covenant.

Once upon a time when religion held life together, those who violated this law of God were hauled into court by religious consciences. The charge was public prostitution—making love to a form.

Sounding for all the world like a street evangelist, the writer of II Timothy called upon his readers to avoid such criminal lovers—those who preserve the form of religion but deny its power. Avoid them? Where could we go? With whom would we sleep? How could we shave or put on makeup without looking into a mirror? Who would answer when our names were called?

We love those sensuous forms of religion. They are so caressable, so photogenic, so "round and firm and fully packed." And if cigarettes can be sold by image, why not God—or, at least, religion?

Perhaps this love of form in religion is not as analogous to prostitution as it is to masturbation—ecclesiastical self-love. Uncertain of God, we determine to love ourselves in the forms of religion—Christians in love with love.

In a small southern town the village simpleton stood beside the railroad tracks every day and waved to the passengers on their way to Florida. "It's embarrassing for the entire town; it's bad for tourism," lamented the town council. But, how to remove this prodigy of shame? After two weeks a duly appointed committee announced a stratagem that would keep the simpleton away from the tracks: he would be given the task of polishing the old Confederate cannon on the courthouse square; there would be a modest stipend, two weeks' vacation, and an ostentatious uniform. The cannon shone brightly in response to the new program of maintenance. Then one day the simpleton appeared before the council to turn in his uniform. "Why?" asked the civic leaders. "Isn't the salary adequate? Don't you enjoy your work?" "Everything's fine," replied the simpleton, "but I've bought some cannons of my own. I'm going in business for myself."

There is glaring evidence that much of what we call religion is primarily cannon-polishing—tender maintenance of the forms which keeps us away from the tracks. *Idolatry* is the biblical label for such worship of form; although biblical writers are more specific.

Religion as "dull habit" was William James' description for dutiful toleration of religious forms. James dashed off to take the temperatures of a variety of persons in order to study religion as an acute fever. Thomas Merton was born too late to participate in James' research, but the Trappist monk had a fever caused by infectious iconoclasm. "Idolatry," reasoned Merton, is "the willingness to give reality to metaphysical nothingness by sacrificing to it." At present it is Western man's sacrifice to "popular religion."

Popular religion has to a great extent betrayed man's inner spirit and turned him over, like Samson, with his hair cut off and his eyes dug out, to turn the mill of a self-frustrating and self-destroying culture. The clichés of popular religion have in many cases become every bit as hollow and as false as those of soap salesmen, and far more dangerously deceptive because one cannot so easily verify the claims made about the product.[1]

[1] Thomas Merton, *Faith and Violence* (Notre Dame, Ind.: University of Notre Dame Press, 1968), pp. 116-17.

What is rumored of mice concerning the absence of authority is also applicable to men: when the gods are away, the people will play—play at religion by shifting all the forms around, play at joy by grinning too much in trouped-up worship, play at love by insisting upon brief, sensual covenants, or, conversely, continue the same old game of "dull habit." T. S. Eliot wrote in his "Choruses from 'The Rock'":

> But it seems that something has happened that has never happened before: though we know not just when, or why, or how, or where.
> Men have left G O D not for other gods, they say, but for no god; and this has never happened before
> That men both deny gods and worship gods, professing first Reason,
> And then Money, and Power, and what they call Life, or Race, or Dialectic,
> The Church disowned, the tower overthrown, the bells upturned, and what have we to do
> But stand with empty hands and palms turned upwards
> In an age which advances progressively backwards?[2]

Standing "with empty hands and palms turned upwards" could be construed as a semblance of

[2] T. S. Eliot, *Collected Poems 1909-1962* (New York: Harcourt Brace Jovanovich, Inc., 1963), pp. 163-64.

receptivity, a sign of waiting. But man is a notoriously poor waiter. His patience wears thin quickly; his ego cannot long endure belated appearances without slipping into mild paranoia. The Old and New Testaments are plethoric with man's unwillingness to wait. The Exodus narrative records a good example: Moses had gone up to the mountains to strike a covenant with God. When the people saw that Moses "delayed," they said to Aaron, "Make us gods." When the gods are away, the people make their own rules, flex their muscles, run about without any restraining leash. In their loneliness they create their own pantheons, with a god to bless "each thought and each motive." Advent is the season of God's scheduled arrival; "you can set your watch by it." Expectancy has been routinized. Surprises are now man-made; religion is merely form. That's the way to run a good railroad.

On the other hand there is copious evidence of a "holy" dissatisfaction with *form*al religion. When Moses descended the mountain and saw the people dancing around the golden calf, "his anger burned hot, and he threw the tables out of his hands and broke them . . . . And he took the calf which they had made, and burnt it with fire, and ground it to powder, and scattered it upon the water, and made the people of Israel drink it" (Exodus 32:19-20).

Prophetic iconoclasm triumphs over the tangible gods that fill all the vacuous "meantimes" of man. "Drink this," says the iconoclast, "it's for your own good." And it is, but what a bitter taste is left in the mouth from swallowing the powdered forms of one's own gods. It is the bitterness of pride.

Thomas Merton chose the Samson saga to illustrate man's bondage to the idols of "popular religion." It was a call for iconoclasts. "The Church betrays herself and modern man if she simply identifies with his superstitions, his image-making, his political snake-handling and his idolatries of nation, party, class and race."[3] Why Samson? Was it mere coincidence, or did Merton intend to call attention to the need for *radical* iconoclasm? "The lords of the Philistines gathered to offer a great sacrifice to Dagon their god, and to rejoice; for they said, 'Our god has given Samson our enemy into our hand '" (Judges 16:23). Samson was brought to the feast and "made sport before them." Finally, in a mighty act of vengeance and worship, the slave Samson, "with his hair cut off and his eyes dug out," pulled the temple of Dagon down upon the worshippers and himself. It was redeeming, the redemption of iconoclasm.

"Progress of religion," wrote Alfred North

[3]Merton, *Faith and Violence*, p. 161.

Whitehead, "is defined by the denunciation of gods." "Pull down the idols from every high hill," cried Old Testament prophets. "Yahweh alone is God." "Hear, O Israel, the Lord our God is one LORD." That's all you need; that's all there is. And even that had to be purged by young Jews from Jesus to Franz Kafka.

The twenty-third chapter of Matthew's Gospel contains poignant evidence of Jesus' iconoclasm; Kafka phrased his in a letter.

> In the synagogue, I could twist and turn about as much as I liked. So I used to yawn and fiddle the long hours away—the only place where I have been as bored later on was, I believe, when I went to dancing lessons. . . . So that was the stuff that was handed on to me to build my faith out of. . . . What better was there to do with such material than get rid of it as quickly as possible I couldn't imagine; in fact, just getting rid of it seemed to me the most godly thing to do with it.[4]

Religious orthodoxy has always been intent upon handing on the "stuff" of faith. A conservative orthodoxy called me saved before I ever really knew what it was to be lost, and my next twenty years were spent in frustrated rebellion. The years were strewn with the discarded "stuff" of or-

[4]Max Brod, *Franz Kafka* (New York: Schocken Books, 1960), pp. 26-27.

thodoxy, strewn by a pilgrim determined to travel light—too light at times. A Roman Catholic, Jean Daniélou, unsealed my orders when he wrote, "A Christian is nothing more than a pagan on the way to conversion." With a little imagination, orthodoxy might allow such a view to be designated "Preface" to a doctrine of Sanctification. No matter. Faith hardly ever stops and starts at orthodox lights anymore.

During the first Holy Week, as reported in the Gospel of John, the disciple Thomas is characterized as "a pagan on the way." He listens to Jesus tell of his imminent departure, saying:

"And you know where I am going."
"Wait a minute, Rabbi," exclaimed Thomas,
"we don't know where you are going, and
how are we supposed to know the way?"
"I am way, truth, and life," declares Jesus.

But the way was abandoned abruptly as a superhighway stops suddenly in the middle of nowhere, waiting for the next government appropriation; the truth was labeled "lie" by the religious establishment; the life was stretched on a cross to dry in the sun, then packed away in a storehouse for skins.

Faith crawled into a hole and pulled the earth in

on it to hide the shame of it all. Behind locked doors the faithful cowered in fright and guilt. They had lost the form of their religion and did not know where to find it. Leave it alone, Blue Boys, and it will come to you again, new and lively.

But Thomas was not there at the homecoming. He had stepped out for a breath of fresh air, and while he was gone the Spirit blew into that stifling room. The others could not help Thomas catch up. They could only give him words, not an experience. Experience cannot be passed from hand to hand, cannot be bottled and sold over the counter, cannot be mimeographed and handed out at the next meeting. Experience has a historical quality. It is *event*ful and is always passing away.

Thomas grabbed the icon that was being molded and dashed it to the floor. He would have none of this superstitious religion. It was not the experience he doubted; it was the witness, the form. The essence of the experience was not Thomas' to doubt or to affirm; he could only doubt what others told him. Hermann Hesse formed this idea in a couple of sentences.

> He who travels far will often see things
> Far removed from what he believed was Truth.
> When he talks about it in the fields at home,
> He is often accused of lying,

For the obdurate people will not believe
What they do not see and distinctly feel.[5]

Experiences are not easily formed, corralled by words. Have you ever watched a well-trained sheep dog herd sheep—running back and forth, yapping and snapping at their heels, moving them gradually toward the pen, racing back to get a stray, drawing them together? In some similar manner words attempt to articulate experiences— running, yelling, stopping abruptly, dashing off in another direction. And, finally, when the job is all done, leaving the sheep to wander out again while they race off down the valley after an almost forgotten stray. The task is never finished in some final, dogmatic way. The creed, no matter how well stated, still has some stray adjectives and verbs. Perhaps e. e. cummings had this in mind when he described God as "a little more than everything."

This holy dissatisfaction with final form is not at all to be confused with cynicism. The cynic has no vested interest; he lets go of old forms too easily, feels no remorse or sense of vacuum, has no questions or doubts; he has only predilections: one who knows the price of everything and the value of nothing. For this reason a cynic could

[5] Hermann Hesse, *The Journey to the East* (New York: Noonday Press, 1970), pp. 7-8.

never be a pilgrim or a "pagan on the way to conversion." If John Bunyan is to be trusted, pilgrimage is toward the light with the shadowy forms falling behind. Bunyan's Evangelist asks Christian at the beginning of the journey:

"Do you see yonder wicket-gate?"

"No," replies Christian.

"Do you see yonder shining light?" persists Evangelist.

Christian strains his eyes and stammers: "I think I do."

"Keep that light in your eye," Evangelist advises.

And often during that exodus, one longs for the security of Plato's cave—life with forms only. To leave the cave was to be blinded by the brilliant sunlight.

Better to "see" essence without sight than to look only on forms all your life. The Venus of Milo has a room all to herself in the Louvre. What a beautiful, graceful form, but I wouldn't want to go to bed with her—a frigid block of marble. No, for loving I'll take the warm reality of my wife. And that full-page foldout in *Playboy?* A paper tiger in bed.

Should religion, then, cast off all form? Become a raging, formless fever? Such questions are little more than romantic rhetoric. Dietrich Bonhoeffer's call for "religionless Christianity" borders on such romanticism.

New skins for new wine—that was Jesus' motto. Some have decided that the best way to follow this injunction is to drink the wine and to discard the old carry-all wine skins. They are near the kingdom.

The form is what we know, what we touch, caress, fondle, kiss, embrace. Yet all this is merely a way to say something to the essence housed in that form: to touch it without manhandling it, to hold it without strangling it, to protect it without smothering it. The form is ours yet not ours—just as the gospel is ours and yet not ours. No, the form does not merely *house* the essence. The relationship is closer, more essential than that. It is precisely not the genie-in-the-bottle analogy—rub the form long enough, with sufficient expectation (faith) and the genie will appear. That's not at all the case in Christianity, despite all the institutional stroking.

The form and the essence are inseparable for any particular time. To encounter essence in a specific form is an experience, a happening. Form is not expendable. God "dies" when formless, dies the death of generalization, oozes out, is soaked up, and gone.

At the same time form is not an end, does not

call attention to itself. Form points beyond itself. It invites one to enter an experience. This is the "broken symbol" of which Tillich wrote. The most adequate symbol deliberately depicts its own inadequacy. Tillich preached: "It is the greatness of Christianity that it can see how small it is. The importance of being a Christian is that we can stand the insight that it is of no importance. It is the spiritual power of religion that he who is religious can fearlessly look at the vanity of religion."[6]

What else but local vanity would lead Christians to establish several congregations within a few blocks of one another, build expensive buildings which will scarcely ever be used efficiently, and then sign on a full-time crew to keep the forms functional? These religious "lies" stand on one corner after another with self-conscious fingers pointing heavenward and that presumptuous epitaph carved in stone above so many locked doors: The House of God. Local vanity, subsidized by denominational forms.

"Well," says some pious soul, "we're all going in the same direction." All the more reason to go together; though I'm not certain that we're going in the same direction. We are more like ships passing in the night.

[6]Paul Tillich, *The New Being* (New York: Charles Scribner's Sons, 1955), p. 19.

There are signs that succeeding generations will have less regard for the luxury of denominational forms. It is likely that religious choices of the future will be made increasingly on the basis of issues, local congregational integrity, concepts of church mission, and ministry. We will need more holy elasticity in our forms, and woe to those who are determined to anchor one end of that elastic band; they're in for one whale of a backlash.

Religion is finding intensive expression in relational activities rather than in orthodox formulae. Men are meeting God "in each Thou," as Buber said. This is not ecumenicity as a leveling-down process, a search for some lowest common denominator. It is believing God rather than believing *in* God, trusting him and all those who worship him, naming the name of God together, experiencing God in broken symbols.

One of the best treatises on the matter of unorthodox relationships is presented in the fifteenth chapter of Luke's Gospel. The chapter opens, "The tax-gatherers and other bad characters were all crowding in to listen to him [Jesus]; and the Pharisees and the doctors of the law began grumbling among themselves: 'This fellow,' they said, 'welcomes sinners and eats with them'" (15:1-2 NEB). Three parables follow this introduction: a shepherd with one hundred sheep leaves ninety-nine of them to search for one stray. When he finds the lost sheep he brings it home, and there is a celebration. The second story tells of a woman who lost one of her ten coins. She searches the house until she finds it, and there is a celebration. The third story pictures a different sort of relationship from the first two. Here, one must pry into personal matters. A father has two sons. After wasting his share of the family fortune, the younger son returns home. His father welcomes him, and there is a celebration. The elder son resents the welcome. He is jealous of his father's lavish display of affection. He has never received such, has never even asked for such. This elder son questions his own acceptability to the father and lays all the blame for this doubt upon his parent.

Luke raises the questions: Why should sinners and outcasts receive equal time with the Father? Why shouldn't the Father's time be confined to Pharisees and doctors of the law? Who has the ear of God?

In Jesus' day they were the Pharisees and doctors of the law, the professional listeners to God, the qualified "forms" that mediated God. Today, they are the Baptists, Presbyterians, Roman Catholics, Episcopalians—the professional religionists. Any group with a corner on the God market.

There are numerous signs in the New Testament

that it did not take the early Christians long to embody this elder-brother syndrome. Christians grew closer and closer to God and farther and farther from their Jewish brothers. What a paradox that! Abraham Heschel wrote, "The children did not arise to call the mother blessed; instead, they called the mother blind."[7] It was more serious, however, than adolescent rebellion manifested in name-calling; the children ran away from home and thought to take the household deity with them.

Could it be that Christians have done precisely what Jews feared might be done, idolized Jesus of Nazareth? Have Christians supplanted God by deifying Jesus, which is actually the opposite of incarnation? Have Christians taken the way to God and made him a dead end, leading nowhere beyond himself? Has this been done because Christians refuse to live with the holy mystery that is God? Finding it so much easier to get our minds around this Jesus, have we settled for a sentimentalized version of God? Remember, Jesus did not come to found a religion; he came to awaken faith in God.[8]

Jesus, according to the testimony of church, brings persons into dynamic relationship with

[7] Abraham Heschel, "No Religion Is an Island," *Union Seminary Quarterly Review* (January 1966), p. 124.

[8] See Gerhard Ebeling's discussion in *The Nature of Faith,* tr. Ronald G. Smith (Philadelphia: Fortress Press, 1962).

God. This Jesus stretched holy elasticity to its breaking point. He raised questions that the orthodox and the unorthodox thought had already been answered—finally. These were not Jewish questions or Christian questions; these were human questions. For too long we have researched questions of dogma and creed, questions of ecclesiastical institutionalism and left off asking what Howard Moody calls "questions which are the womb out of which faith is born." For too long questions have not pushed against the boundaries of religious form. The push is now on.

II.
Religion: Song or Dance

Singing and dancing have been deliberately separated in the United States. One sings *or* dances. The closest I come to a real song and dance is the Sunday morning procession and recession, if wobbling from side to side and lurching from note to note can be properly termed a song and dance. It was certainly the intention of those early religious processions—genuine dances up to and around the altar, singing and shouting all the way.

Discounting imported folk dances, I recall only one other instance of a union between singing and dancing in the United States; it occurred in those movie musicals of the late 1930s and early 1940s. While dancing with a partner, the star would suddenly begin to sing. Right there in the middle of the dance floor, singing away, and the other dancers only smiled or failed to notice. Try *that* the next time you're on the dance floor!

No, we Americans don't sing and dance at the same time which has caused me to envy European singing folk dancers. It's a pity that we have so drastically separated these art forms.

Perhaps it is more than coincidence, a style of life even, the overcompartmentalization of life— dance *or* sing, good *or* bad, cops *or* robbers, cowboys *or* Indians, white *or* black, Protestant *or* Roman Catholic. I know of two church buildings that are back to back, separated by an Anchor fence to keep Methodists from straying over on Presbyterian property or vice versa. It is a distinct way to live. "Good fences make good neighbors."

How upsetting when someone leaves the doors of our compartments open and interchange occurs. Roman Catholics wander over on Protestant turf; blacks shatter treasured white prejudices by their similarities of hopes and goals.

In 1956 I moved from the South to New York City for graduate school. During the twenty-five years of my life, I had never known a black person who wasn't an unskilled laborer or a tenant farmer. My wife and I were invited to a social gathering in Harlem—mostly blacks with a seasoning of international students. The first black with whom I talked at length was a woman schoolteacher, just slightly older than myself. My inter-

nal audio-visual had her stooping in a kindergar-
ten class pointing to the puppies and kitties on the
pages of brightly colored books. "What do you
teach?" I inquired. "Latin and Russian," she
responded. I'd never had one day's instruction in
either, and my audio-visual equipment shorted
out. The door of one of my compartments swung
freely on its hinges.

This attempt to compartmentalize life is our
desire to control. Unable to control the whole, life
is divided into manageable segments. This is sin
and is reflected in the forms of religion as in all
other forms of life.

For example, the forms of religion have evi-
denced an inordinate separation between belief
and action. Whole generations have wasted hours
and days of prime time in endless discussion on
the nature of Christ or the mission of the church.
While countless other generations have acted
frenetically in the name of a god who does not
even exist. It is singing *or* dancing.

For the religious quietist, stress is placed upon
proper cultic response to divinity. Religion is
proper forms in worship and proper content in
education. How wonderful and reassuring it is for
the brothers and sisters to gather regularly at the
church building for religious discussions and
study groups on world missions, but if the
discussion threatens to spill over into action,

especially some form of controversial social action, religious quietists close their Bibles and go home. They threaten permanent withdrawal and cancellation of financial pledges, the way a young neurotic wife threatened to go home to Mama when things were not going to suit her (or a young neurotic husband withdrew into the TV for the same reason). Religious quietists can remember "when the sanctuary was filled with worshipers," and they imply that the same would be true if the Board of Missions were not composed of radicals.

The religious activists, on the other hand, *demand* action on behalf of others. The cry is to help *them* who usually live in some far-off ghetto (what did we do before we popularized that heavenly hellish word?). This demand for action is not always the outgrowth of one's belief. One church member declared, "I don't know what I believe about Jesus, but I am sure going to help my neighbors." This sister had something for the ghetto that she could not share with the person who sat beside her on the pew.

There are inside activists and outside activists. The inside activists spend most of their time oiling the machinery of the church's "programs" which is a whir of activity since these inside activists have voted "to keep the lights burning for God"—the eternal flame for Protestants. Every week I received a church newspaper that tired me merely to read it. It reeked of successful religious activity. How could a clergyman promote all that, crow about it by smearing adjectives all over every page, and at the same time preserve his integrity? One week a letter came from this pusher indicating that he was contemplating a vocational change. A month later there was this note: "Free at last. Free at last. Thank God, I'm free at last." When church activism has no soul, lacks integrity, it is merely a propaganda form. How I have ached with the strain of keeping all the props in place, made my rounds dutifully, and punched the clock at each check point the way an efficient night watchman should, or I have become a full-time maintenance man—the super who keeps the drains unclogged, the light bulbs in, the floors scrubbed. And on my rounds I have bumped into others of the clerical union. The danger is that the clergy will become chief of the inside activists.

The outside activists scatter from the gathered community like small children at an Easter egg hunt, searching for bright opportunities of religious activity. They are going where the action is, as though God no longer acts in his gathered people or in the service of worship. These outside activists quickly lose patience with the foot-dragging insiders and tend to go it alone, with only God to guide them, if he can keep up.

How we needed the word and style from those

strange prophets—the flower children, the hippies—a reminder of the ease with which religious activity becomes an idol. "Don't just do something, stand there," wasn't that the word? Some Westerners begrudge that contented smile on the big, fat buddha's face. "Grab him up and force him into some ghetto, that will wipe the smile from his face."

To believe *or* to act, to sing *or* to dance? It's the *or* that is wrong, that keeps holding apart what belongs together. Jung wrote: "The opposites always balance on the scales—a sign of high culture. One-sidedness, though it lends momentum, is a mark of barbarism."[1]

The American church reeled out of the 1950s, inebriated by its own success. There were elegant worship bulletins sporting flattering pictures of elaborate church structures and underneath it all the pious cliché, "Every visitor a welcome guest." Then one day, as the 1950s were fading, some black visitors stepped up to the door and called the church's bluff. A new ecclesiastical welcome mat was needed—less demanding, more restrictive, something like, "Every white Anglo-Saxon Protestant a welcome guest." Robert Rodenmayer illustrated the point with an experience from his days as a seminary student. A seminarian, ordained

[1] C. G. Jung, *Psychological Reflections,* ed. Jolande Jacobi (New York: Harper & Brothers, 1953), p. 129.

during his last semester, dressed in his black suit, his gleaming white collar, his well-polished shoes, contemplated himself in the mirror. Pleased with what he saw, he decided to deprive the world of his services no longer and went forth to do God's bidding on Ninth Avenue in New York City. As he stood on the curb, hands in pockets, wondering what to do, he was observed by a drunk who seemed unimpressed. Their eyes met and the drunk said, "Sonny, what the hell do you know about God?" The young man made no reply, went to his room, removed his clerical garb, and wondered what the hell he did know about God.[2]

There is hopeful evidence that church is surrendering her illusion of grandeur, laying aside her arrogance. It is a form of self-defrocking. Our bluff has been called. The splendor of church has been unveiled. "Thank God for that," wrote Paul to the Corinthians. Now, he continued, we are able to behold the glory of the Lord "with unveiled face...."

It was once more that ancient story of Moses' ascent of the sacred mountain, when the people saw that his face shone with the glory of the Lord. Moses was unaware of his shining face, as all genuinely holy men are. Informed of this phenomenon, he covered his face with a veil while meeting with the people, removing it only when

[2]Robert N. Rodenmayer, *We Have This Ministry* (New York: Harper & Brothers, 1959), p. 108.

he went before the Lord. How I admired that story as a child. This great man of God veiled himself to keep from embarrassing those who were not as close to God as he. He would not flaunt his holiness. Then one day I stumbled upon Paul's account of this incident. The apostle to the Gentiles ripped off Moses' mask, and on that day I buried Moses, my hero, and came to love and to sympathize with Moses, the man. Later, even Cecil B. DeMille could not idolize my Moses; Paul had shown too much of his human side. Moses wore his veil, wrote Paul, "so that the Israelites might not see the end of the fading splendor" (II Cor. 3:13). Moses had spent a high moment with God, the splendor of a shining face, the evidence of presence, and he did not want the community to know when that presence had faded.

Hypocrites the Greeks labeled it, a "stage player." "The church is filled with hypocrites." Actors! Certainly! All the world's a stage, including church, and what is liturgy if not *action* of the people? It was Kierkegaard who upset a prevalent understanding of worship by putting the worshipers in the roles of actors who played before God while the preacher prompted them.

What's the difference between an actor in the high school play and one in a Broadway drama? The high school player tries to repeat memorized lines without forgetting them; the Broadway actor becomes the part he is playing. The Christian believer is a professional actor.

One Sunday following a worship service in which I had been the visiting preacher, a man whom I had not seen since college days invited me to his home for lunch. During the afternoon we did what all southerners did in the 1960s; we talked about civil rights. My friend was a lawyer, and he told me of a legal society luncheon at which he was seated next to a black lawyer from New York. After the salad the black northerner turned to the white southerner and asked, "How does it feel to be eating next to a Negro?" My friend replied, "It's about to make me sick to my stomach. But, then, I'm a Christian, and my guts will just have to get used to it." There's an actor becoming a part, getting his belief and his action together. "O God, keep our mouths from saying what our hearts do not believe."

It is a question of focus. In 1937 Auden wrote:

> Preserve me from the Shape of Things to Be;
>   The high-grade posters at the public meeting,
> The influence of Art on Industry,
>   The cinemas with perfect taste in seating;
>   Preserve me, above all, from central heating.
> It may be D. H. Lawrence hocus-pocus,
> But I prefer a room that's got a focus.[3]

[3]W. H. Auden, "Letter to Lord Byron," *Collected Longer Poems* (New York: Random House, 1969), p. 47.

Have you ever tried to warm your posterior by backing up to electric heat—in the ceiling? Perhaps this is a prime reason for so much contemporary frustration. Generations are maturing in centrally heated environments, the source of energy cleverly disguised. Auden thought it wise to know his benefactor in focused appreciation.

Church is always tempted to set the underbrush on fire then gather around some burning bush to listen for the word of God. Uncertain of any source of energy, we ecclesiastical madmen leap into the world's marketplaces asking with Nietzsche, "Must we not light lanterns at noonday?"

To an earlier generation of believers, P. T. Forsyth counseled: "We have to dwell much with the everlasting burnings of God's love. We have to tend that consuming fire. We have to feed our life where all the tragedy of life is gathered to an infinite and victorious crisis in Christ. We are not the fire, but we live where it burns."[4]

The early disciples of Jesus lived where the fire was burning; they knew themselves to be "strangely warmed" in the focus of faith.[5] Then suddenly the fire was doused, and they were left with a stifling smoke that filled their lungs and

[4] P. T. Forsyth, *The Soul of Prayer*, (London: The Independent Press, 1949), p. 73.

[5] In *Individual Dream Symbolism in Relation to Alchemy*, C. G. Jung cites an uncanonical saying of Jesus, "He who is near unto me is near unto the fire." See *The Portable Jung* (New York: Viking Press, p. 376).

seared their eyes. They had backed up to a very specific fire of God, had lived in that warmth, and when it was out they knew it.

"I'm going back to the fishing business," Simon mourned. Business was fair to poor. When the fish were running and Simon pulled the nets until his arms ached and his mind was filled with work, it was all right. But when there were no fish and the boat rocked gently in the breeze with the waves slapping rhythmically against the side, it was hell. Memory kept racing off to those days of preaching and teaching and healing. A fire had raged through the countryside, and he had been a spark of it. Now the fire was out, the sparks scattered, and a hard day's rain was falling on the land.

One morning on the beach beside the Sea of Tiberias, Simon was confronted by the risen Christ who asked, "Simon, son of John, do you love me more than these?" "Yes, Lord," declared the fisherman. "Feed my sheep," commanded Christ. Belief and action were brought together into one sharp image—the way a camera is in focus when subject is superimposed upon subject. The focus is worship–service, God–neighbor.

Luther called it *Gottesdienst*, God serving the worshiper and vice versa. Most of us in the Protestant tradition still refer to a specific time of the week as "worship service." Yet, the past two decades have been flooded with the heresy that one gathers to worship and scatters to serve.

One month of a Georgia spring spent in a Trappist monastery laid this spiritual schizophrenia to rest finally for me. The brothers served and worshiped as surely as any revivalist, inner-city reformer, or establishment ecclesiast that I have ever known. For me the experience was a saving wholeness, the realization that whoever separates worship and service neither worships nor serves. Of course, we needed that catchy reminder from Robert Spike that the church was "of the world but not in the world." We needed the call to marketplace theology, needed to be called out of stained-glass sanctuaries into sensuous shopping centers. Yet, response was fractured, a cartoon cowboy jumping on his horse and riding off in all directions at the same time.

The reminder that church is a celebrative people came as an integrative vitality: church in the marketplace, celebrating, or more radical, playing. Wasn't this the imagery some early Christians found helpful in depicting a call to discipleship? Two groups of children were sitting in a marketplace (Matt. 11:16-19). One group shouts to the other, "We played wedding music for you, but you would not dance! We sang funeral songs, but you would not mourn!" It is not a question of polarization—one group wanting to play wedding while the other wishes to play funeral. One group does all the shouting, offers to play anything from wedding to funeral. The game is the thing; it does not matter which game. The other children refuse to play anything. John the Baptist came as an austere ascetic; Jesus came as a joyful teacher, but most of the people in the marketplaces of Palestine refused to play either game.

Does not the misery of the world's marketplaces nullify all play? How can we play when children starve and men kill one another in wars? How can we play when the air we breathe and the water we drink are saturated with pollution? W. H. Auden offers an answer to these questions in his poem, "Death's Echo." The first stanza concludes:

> The earth is an oyster with nothing inside it,
>   Not to be born is the best for man;
> The end of toil is a bailiff's order,
>   Throw down the mattock and dance while you can.[6]

Right in the midst of a sad and anxious world, church is called to sing and dance.

One recent autumn, the Thanksgiving Day parade in our city was selected for national television viewing. There were two problems: (1) the parade, customarily held in the afternoon, would have to be on Thanksgiving morning; (2) a

[6]Auden, "Death's Echo," *Collected Shorter Poems* (New York: Random House, 1966), p. 103.

number of churches customarily scheduled worship services for the morning of Thanksgiving Day. Community debates filled the mass media of communication. Which should yield? Marketplace *or* sanctuary, good *or* evil, God *or* Satan? Then someone suggested, "Perhaps God loves a parade, would prefer sitting on the curb to a similar position on the altar."

Why was it such a novel idea? Why is God supposed to be so humorless? A psalmist believed that the Lord laughs at the wicked because he foresees their downfall. Some joke if you're wicked. But at least God is depicted with a sense of humor even if it is a bit warped. Do you recall Sarah, wife of Abraham? She named her son Laughter (Isaac) since bearing a child at her advanced age was really a joke. It was God who turned Sarah's joke into the lasting joy of covenant, and Sarah celebrated when action and belief were brought to focus. "God has made laughter for me," she sang. Standing in the anteroom to the morgue, it was God who enabled Sarah to "throw down the mattock and dance" while she could. These celebrations come in the midst of life's trials, in the marketplaces; joy and sorrow, weeping and laughing, mourning and dancing comingled.

When I was a small schoolboy, we sang a silly song about "Charming Billy."

Oh, where have you been, Billy Boy, Billy Boy,
   Oh, where have you been, charming Billy?
I have been to seek a wife,
   She's the joy of my life,
She's a young thing and cannot leave her mother.

Verse after verse extolled the virtues of this girl.

   She can bake a cherry pie
   Quick's a cat can wink her eye.

But, always, "She's a young thing and cannot leave her mother." It is the ambiguity of celebration.

Wandering in the wilderness the people of God knew the freedom from slavery and the loneliness of independence; languishing in exile they knew the presence of God in a strange land and the absence of familiar religion. Their children eat bitter herbs at the Passover celebration and the latter-day saints of this movement break bread as a symbol of Messiah's broken body and drink wine as a reminder of his blood and call it *celebration* of Holy Communion.

"Now, no joy but lacks salt," reflected Robert Frost,

   That is not dashed with pain,
   And weariness and fault;
   I crave the stain
   Of tears, the aftermark

> Of almost too much love,
> The sweet of bitter bark
> And burning clove.[7]

There is irrefutable evidence that Western religious tradition has attempted to breed out all ambiguity, to attain the purity of "best of show." The pure line was sacred, saint, Sunday, without the bastardly element of secular, sinner, and Saturday night. The Protestant Reformers appear to have been overzealous about their work. The church was not only reformed, it was bulldogged to the ground and branded. Bishop James Pike used to say, "While John Calvin didn't get rid of sin, he sure took the joy out of it." The magnificent organ was removed from the Grossmünster in Zurich, hewn in pieces, and thrown into the Limmat River; then, the walls were whitewashed to cover the beauty of the distracting frescoes. It was the unwillingness to live with the hybrid. It was the senility of those who forgot that Jesus was in trouble constantly due to his association with *half*-breeds.

Shall we never learn that scheduled celebrations cannot fulfill unambiguous expectations, that traveling sales representatives will never experience the full joy they anticipated upon their arrival

[7]"To Earthward," *The Poetry of Robert Frost*, ed. Edward Connery Lathem (New York: Holt, Rinehart and Winston, 1969), p. 227.

home on Friday afternoon, that Christmas cannot possibly bear the weight of hopeful joy for more than a few minutes? One Christmas I received a homemade card from a former student and his wife. At the top was a scripture verse.

> He will cause the bright dawn of salvation to rise on us, and shine on all those who live in the dark shadow of death.

In the center of the card was a piece of torn, crumpled paper with gray and black and green marks on it. Under the paper this statement, "We've been slowly mending since the death of our baby in June."

Those early Christians leaned heavily upon something that we seem to have forgotten: God is trustworthy; his is the power and the glory and the kingdom for ever and ever. How improbable it is that we shall ever hear institutional faith laughing in the face of very serious budget campaigns, building drives, and missions designed to save the whole world in the 1970s. Yet, in the very act of my pious prayers, I could swear that I have sometimes heard God say, "Aww-w, throw down the mattock and dance while you can."

How to laugh at ourselves—that would be a lesson well worth learning, and we could not find a better instructor than the most serious dogmatic theologian of the twentieth century, Karl Barth.

While writing weighty and lengthy tomes on church dogmatics, Barth penned these words.

> The angels laugh at old Karl. They laugh at him because he tries to grasp the truth about God in a book of Dogmatics. They laugh at the fact that volume follows volume and each is thicker than the previous one. As they laugh, they say to one another, "Look! Here he comes now with his little pushcart full of volumes of the *Dogmatics!*" [8]

What a celebrative humility that is—the recognition of one's stance before God, laughter at homemade attempts at salvation.

We could use another Will Rogers in the United States. Will helped people laugh at everything—the church, the congress, the president. Today, Will Rogers would likely be investigated as a subversive.

A primary deficiency in radical militants of both left and right is their inability to laugh at themselves; they are too intense. They are certain that the salvation of society rests in their hands. History has taught us to be wary of self-conscious messiahs with their inflated claims. Remember the Christian missionary challenge of the early twentieth century? Save the world in our generation. It was no laughing matter. That was its inadequacy,

[8] George Casalis, *Portrait of Karl Barth* (Garden City, N. Y.: Doubleday & Company, Inc., 1963), p. 3.

the inadequacy of much of the modern mission enterprise. Once I overheard an American missionary lamenting the sad state of religious affairs in England. Another missionary, a Southern Baptist, blurted out, "I could take two Southern Baptist evangelists from Texas and save the whole damn British Isles in a ten-day revival meeting." It was a laughing at oneself.

In the Horatio Alger approach to life, celebration is reserved as a reward for work well done; it is a heaven at last; a gold watch after years and years of meritorious service. Now, however, there are signs that the church is determined to risk a "singing in the rain", celebration as a style of life, singing *and* dancing in the world.

Auden concludes his poem, "Death's Echo":

> The desires of the heart are as crooked as corkscrews,
>   Not to be born is the best for man;
> The second-best is a formal order,
>   The dance's pattern; dance while you can.
>
> Dance, dance, for the figure is easy,
>   The tune is catching and will not stop;
> Dance till the stars come down from the rafters;
>   Dance, dance, dance till you drop.[9]

[9] Auden, "Death's Echo," p. 104.

III.
Religion: Fact or Fiction

A small boy gave the following summary of his Sunday school lesson.

"There were these Jews who had broken out of a prison camp in Egypt. They ran and ran until they came to a wide lake. The prison guards were closing in so the Jews jumped into the water and swam out to some boats that were waiting for them. The guards got in submarines and tried to torpedo the boats, but the Jews set off depth charges and blew up all the submarines and made it safe to the other side. Everybody called the Admiral by his first name, Moses."

The boy's father asked, "Son, are you certain that's what your teacher told you?"

"Dad," responded the boy, "if you can't believe my story, you'd never believe the one the teacher told."

My grandmother would not have understood the boy's dilemma. In simplistic fashion she always said, "I believe the Bible from cover to cover, every word of it." Grandmother was bragging, not complaining. But then, her faith had not been tampered with. With me, it was a different matter.

The United States was almost a decade beyond a great economic depression when I received my first really nice Bible. It was a leather-bound, gilt-edged, red-letter edition, with my name printed on the front in gold. "Red-letter edition" meant that one possessed the mind of Christ in living color. Thirty years and hours of critical study later, I have discovered from "the educated ones" that it is not so easy to decipher the exact words of our Lord from all the faith-witness that surround them. The early Christians had a way of enhancing what they remembered; faith tended to be all red letter. The facts of the case are difficult to ascertain. They are subsumed in concern for *the fact*. There are too many sets of fingerprints on early faith for us to be absolutely certain about much that we read. The "faith" has been handed down by so many generations, handled and worn smooth in so many marketplaces of the world, set to such different rhythms and expressed in such diverse doctrines, that it has to be held in some humble reverence today. Believers must evidence a holy reluctance to place too much credence in the "forms" of God.

In his *Letters and Papers from Prison*, Dietrich Bonhoeffer articulated what many still feel. "Surely there has never been a generation in the course of human history with so little ground under its feet as our own." [1]

It was not always this way. We were given all sorts of ground when we started our faith-pilgrimage forty or fifty years ago, but it kept sinking beneath our feet, or we sold it off to pay expenses of a higher education, or due to the lack of cultivation it grew up in weeds, and we could never find it again. Gone.

Have you ever read the ancient story of Naaman the leper in II Kings 5? He was a commander in the Syrian army who had a captive Hebrew maid in his household. She had the audacity to advise Naaman to ask an Israelite prophet, Elisha, to cure his leprosy. At the end of his frayed rope, Naaman took the maid's advice and unraveled himself toward Israel. Elisha sent his servant out to tell the

[1] Dietrich Bonhoeffer, *Letters and Papers from Prison* (New York: The MacMillan Co., 1965), p. 16.

Syrian commander to go wash in the River Jordan. Naaman was quite disappointed; the advice was too simple; the cure did not seem sufficiently religious. He said, "I thought that the prophet would surely come out to me, and stand, and call on the name of the Lord his God, and wave his hand over the place, and cure the leper." Nevertheless, at the insistence of his advisers, the Syrian followed the prophet's instructions and was cured. He praised God, saying, "I know that there is no God in all the earth but in Israel." Then Naaman made a strange request, "I pray you, let me have two mules's burden of earth; for henceforth your servant will not offer burnt offering or sacrifice to any god but the Lord." The gods were thought to be restricted territorially and in order to worship a particular god, you needed some of his ground on which to kneel or stand.

Most of my life has been spent discarding religious dirt, seeing how many gods I could denounce. Now, I am searching for a place to stand. Listen to what Saul Bellow says.

But what is the philosophy of this generation? Not God is dead, that point was passed long ago. Perhaps it should be stated Death is God. This generation thinks—and this is its thought of thoughts—that nothing faithful, vulnerable, fragile can be durable or have any true power. Death waits for these things ·as a cement floor waits for a dropping light bulb.[2]

In the darkness we pick our way barefoot through the shattered glass on life's cement floor, hoping for the return of durability, for a solid rock on which to build.

Life has been stripped down to what Nietzsche called its *ipsissimosity*—"the bare object"—the essence without form to hide it. Believers have discarded all the clothing of their beliefs, have run naked through the streets of Secular Cities. Religious intelligence claims to have outgrown theological clothing—split britches that were too small, burst binding girdles of fundamentalism, and, in a dazzling ode to freedom, danced right out of all encompassing imagery into an honest nudity with nothing to conceal. Onlookers who once asked about our clothing and wondered about our style, no longer ask or wonder, for in our nudity we resemble all other men. The art of striptease is knowing what to conceal and for how long. Overindulgence of nudity rapidly satiates curiosity.

Perhaps we didn't outgrow our theological clothing at all, nothing so expansive as that. Perhaps they were discarded as unfashionable, left for the Salvation Army, literally. A change of

[2]Saul Bellow, *Herzog* (New York: Viking Press, 1967), pp. 289-90.

clothing—or no clothing at all—we thought, might improve the character of our faith.

Whatever the reason, we still stand naked in the street. We can regret our plight, but not our pilgrimage. We had an awful case of religious constipation—clogged with dishonest, overly naïve piosity—and honesty was a cleansing enema. Yes, we did dance down the hospital corridors and out into the streets with that obscene hospital gown flapping in the breeze. We didn't eat again for months—sipped the frothy elixir of recently discovered liberty, a whole boatload of immigrants delivered to the shore of a new world.

There has been a generation or more of dissuaders who knew precisely what they did not believe—could not believe—ever again. And we needed them; church needed them; Christianity needed them. Some still have not changed any clothing; they wear two-hundred-dollar business suits yet come to religion in bib overalls reeking of agrarianism. They resemble children who have been told over and over, "There are no such things as ghosts." "We know," they reply, shivering beneath their blankets. Dissuasion is still needed, but not as a substitute for faith.

What was given to us anyway? Who packed our lunch when we started on this journey to God? In his pathetic "Letter to My Father," Franz Kafka admonishes his father for his bungling attempts to pass on a faith to his son that he himself did not possess. Kafka wrote:

> Fundamentally the faith that guided your life was that you believed in the absolute rightness of the opinions of a certain class of Jewish businessmen, and really, since these opinions were part of your origin, it was but belief in yourself. There was enough Judaism in that, too, but as far as your child was concerned, it was not enough to be passed on, it trickled away drop by drop as you tried to hand it on.[3]

Kafka's father endeavored to hang on to nostalgia. He paraded out the words that he had memorized, but they were only crushed, faded flowers pressed between the pages of some holy book.

As a relatively new member of the Union of Professional Preachers Local 28207, I keep having this nightmare every Saturday night. I am standing in the pulpit, suspended between heaven and earth, properly robed, and somewhat prepared. When I lift my eyes from my sermon manuscript, all the pews are empty. Then from somewhere comes a great mass of voices singing:

> Thanks—for the memory,
> Of Sunday school and Golden Rule,

[3] Max Brod, *Franz Kafka* (New York: Schocken Books, 1960), p. 28.

54

Of Father, Son, and Spirit, too;
We thank you so much.

Perhaps I have watched too many Bob Hope shows, but the nightmare persists.

We should have learned from the disciple Thomas that experience, no matter how valid, cannot be passed on intact. Forms can be given, and they can be held to the ear, and perhaps the rushing of the sea *will be* heard, but the sound, whatever it is, is a far cry from standing on the shore with the salt breeze in your face and the wet sand beneath your feet. Who will take us to the beach instead of giving us seashells?

Religion is man's passion to experience— Michael Novak's "ultimate drive," Paul Tillich's "ultimate concern." It is a way to transcend the limitations of our finiteness, to stand outside ourselves (ecstasy). That's what the religious pilgrimage is all about. It is not theological schizophrenia, but holy dissatisfaction. Roman Catholics have aspired to the beatific vision; Methodists have longed for sanctification. It is the passion to experience God in the most intense way possible. Quest, pilgrimage, revival, reformation, renewal—a reaching out to apprehend God's revelation.

Far better to have searched and failed to find than never to have searched at all, better the lean, hard sinews of a searcher than a blob of blubbery religious sentimentality, better to have lived with God's absence than to have yelled through a thousand bullhorns, "Here he is!" "There he is!" better to have lived in the agonizing fear that there might be no God at all than to have spewed religious hypocrisies all over the reality of life. James Baldwin testified:

> To be with God is really to be involved with some enormous, overwhelming desire, and joy, and power which you cannot control, which controls you. I conceive of my own life as a journey toward something I do not understand, which in the going toward, makes me better.[4]

Too many have interpreted Jesus' words to Thomas ("Blessed are those who have not seen and yet believe") as discouragement of a tenacious search. A well-intentioned Sunday school teacher once answered a question by declaring, "There are some things God didn't intend for us to know." Things? It isn't things I want to know; it's *God*!

How are we to believe those who say they know God yet appear to have ended their search long ago or never to have begun? How are we to criticize those who keep discarding clothing or mules's burdens of dirt, who question and doubt

4James Baldwin, *Nobody Knows My Name* (New York: Dell Books, 1961), p. 113.

what others have never considered worth inves-
tigating? Are most afraid to do research in
religion, afraid of what they might find or might
not find? Are we like those small children who
view frightening television programs through
their fingers—wanting to see but afraid to look?

The search goes on. It seems that God has just
left all the places in which we seek him. We look
on top of sacred mountains covered by fire and
smoke—God is no longer there. We look inside the
ark of the covenant housed in a flappy tent—he
has already left. We look in the holy of holies
hidden in the bowels of the glorious temple—God
is not there. We take a hundred trips to the Holy
Land, loaded with cameras, in hopes of catching a
glimpse of God—no luck. "Where is God?" we
shout in our frustration. We have seen his star in a
million nights; we have heard his name in a
thousand prayers. Are the stars only figments of
our desires and all the prayers stillborn? Religion
for a searcher-after-God is similar to some
second-rate western movie. Riding for days and
days through a hundred different towns, asking
for God in each of them, always to get the same
reply, "He just passed through a couple of days
ago." Seeing the trail plainly there before us,
talking with witnesses who say they have actually
been riding with him, pushing on again, hungry
and thirsty, certain that we shall die before we

catch up with him. Then one day with our eyes glued to the trail, stumbling headlong into a man named Jesus, standing there in the footprints of God! Is this the end of our search? We had expected much more, something a bit more spectacular. Perhaps this Jesus can be reformed to resemble our dream of God. A dash of stardust here and there, a magic wand, a tall silk hat, some brightly colored scarves. Voilá! Our kind of God.

Too many Christian searchers staked out their claim around this Jesus, announced that this was the end of their search, the pot at the end of the rainbow. They drank too much rotgut and slobbered their affections all over this Jesus. Stood back only slightly, admiring how he had grown in wisdom and stature and in favor with God and man, especially man. They allowed as how he was a fine example of Western manhood, the kind of man, in fact, that you'd like your sister to marry. And this Jesusology is not yet dead and may never be.

Biblical criticism challenges this sentimental idolatry. It protests lazy literalistic interpretations of the biblical messages. It is a literary technique that reflects the integrity of the biblical interpreter's passion for truth. The method has, however, never had unanimous endorsement; in fact, some Christians acted as though the critics were panning a novel written by our Lord himself. If the

Bible speaks of the sun moving, then these superbelievers endorse John Jacob Jasper's famous sermon, "De Sun Do Move!"

Actually, biblical narratives display only a secondary interest in historical accuracy. Most of the writers were preachers not historians. "Facts" were never allowed to make a good story boring. Ancient history was not written critically; accounts were freely embellished and then attributed to outstanding persons in order to give them more credence. Historical "facts" might be recovered in a biblical narrative, but if so, it is only by chance. Professor John Knox said on more than one occasion that faith can aid us in the interpretation of the meaning of history, but not in the recovery of the facts of history.

This does not imply a nonchalant attitude toward history. The church didn't ask me to read Williston Walker's *History of the Christian Church* for nothing. Criticism is the church's way of separating truth from falsehood; it is not, however, willing to have *truth* and *fact* used synonymously. It was the church's passion to know which led to the institution of the *advocatus diaboli*. When a proposal is made to canonize a saint, a devil's advocate is appointed by the church. This faithful believer, as an act of duty, searches out all the opposing considerations and states them as persuasively as possible. Thank God for all those amateur devil's advocates who have helped us weed our theological gardens from time to time.

Joined with this passion to know is the more consuming obsession for ecstacy (*ek-stasis*—"to stand outside of"). Men have wandered in and out of temples and churches, stumbled in and out of alcohol, drugs, and the Lord's Supper, slunk in and out of whorehouses and all-American families, prayed, wept, laughed, sung, danced, seeking ways to transcend finiteness. "Projection," sneered Freud; "opiate," mocked Marx; "salvation," declare the believers.

The Preacher (Ecclesiastes) wrote, God "has put eternity into man's mind." We are part of a brass ring which vibrates throughout when struck at any point. Faith is resonance. God struck certain chords in history that set persons vibrating. The waves of vibration continue and set up other vibrations in sympathetic believers.

We read or hear of happenings that stir our imagination and elicit trust and obedience. In this way faith-events are repeatable. Already we have established that experiences are historically limited; yet, they can re-occur by faith-as-resonance in the sympathetic memory and/or imagination of the believer. I *know* what is meant not because I was *there* but because event is *here:* blood sprinkled on the doorpost, exodus from slavery, crucifixion-resurrection, chords vibrating. And

60

the story becomes *our* story, and the song *our* song.

We are participants in the human condition, not merely grammarians of human language. The words we might not recognize always; the condition we know. Thornton Wilder depicts a human disaster in *The Bridge of San Luis Rey*. Five persons are flung to their deaths when the bridge collapses. Why, wonders Wilder at the outset, did this tragedy happen when it did? Why did it happen to these specific persons? What are the facts in the case? Was it the hand of God? The choice of man? Only bad luck or fate? I know only what the author tells me of this event, know these persons only as he describes them, but the situation starts vibrations in me. In the very last paragraph of the novel, Madre María muses:

Soon we shall die and all memory of those five will have left the earth, and we ourselves shall be loved for a while and forgotten. But the love will have been enough; all those impulses of love return to the love that made them. Even memory is not necessary for love. There is a land of the living and a land of the dead and the bridge is love, the only survival, the only meaning.[5]

[5] Thornton Wilder, *The Bridge of San Luis Rey* (New York: Time Inc. Book Division, 1963), pp. 138-39.

The impulse of love is a *fact* of the human condition; it is an ultimate drive. For example, the biblical story of the woman taken in adultery was probably not a fact of the writer's original account; it was inserted later by other hands; nevertheless, we vibrate to the humanity in this story. The religious leaders dragged a woman to Jesus and cast her down at his feet. They said, "Teacher, for some time we have suspected this woman of adultery. Now, we have caught her in the very act. Our law says that she should be stoned. What do you say?" The teacher stooped and scribbled in the sand. Then, finally, he stood and said to them, "You are right. You *religious* people are *always* right. Therefore, you take her and stone her." The religious leaders were concerned with words, with dogmas, with forms. Jesus was interested in the resonance of relationship. Those who brought the woman realized that they were not as religious as they had thought. They dropped their stones and walked away. Jesus asked the woman, "Where are the ones who accused you?" She answered, "No one condemns me now." And then Jesus said, "Neither do I condemn you. But, daughter, your body was not created for that sort of existence. Don't be trapped again." The vibrations are relational.

Truth as personal relationship is a dynamic experience that stands outside pure predictability or matter-of-factness. Anyone who has been in love is aware of this. It is love as unfulfilled promise that makes for the excitement and frustration of relationship. Personal relationships are mysterious; they have no red-letter editions, no *sure* things, no gods without admixture of mystery and myth. Apparently, many who encountered Jesus in the "days of his flesh" clamored for some irrefutable signs of his identity. They wanted to experience God empirically. Helmut Thielicke says they wanted "God's autograph" to show their children, to flash before their friends and enemies proof of God's existence and of their proximity with him. These men found it impossible to see or to hear God in this Jesus. Why wouldn't he give factual answers to their questions? Why all the riddles, or was he merely another preacher playing fast and loose with facts?

This search for certainty was a partial motivation for the "quest of the historical Jesus": the attempt to learn where he lived, the names of his disciples, exactly what he said and did. Then all these historical facts could be pasted together, and we would have God in a collage. With this ecclesiastical manual we could always ask ourselves, "What would Jesus do?" And the perfect answer could be found by consulting chapter 18, verse 24, line 307. These facts would enable us to "walk where Jesus walked"; they would lead us directly to the actual event, without any interpretation, without any doubt, and without any faith. This is the Lord which the day has made.

Upon reading a faith-story in the Bible, the Westerner most often asks "Did it happen?" "Is it true?" The Easterner, from whose environment these stories came originally, asks, "What is the truth in this story?" There is a vast difference. One question is static, the other dynamic; one is factual, the other mysterious; one is closed, the other open.

One of religion's most disastrous mistakes has been the attempt to legalize, codify, credalize. Creeds regiment, tailor the person to fit the suit. Creedal religion too often takes the form of an old writing exercise for children: a few letters or words were made at the top of the child's page, and laboriously he set out to copy them line upon line. Dynamic Christianity has never expressed itself as some ecclesiastical Xerox machine.

Even worse, a creed implies a finished character to religion and faith that too easily becomes assent to a static formula. Much of the excitement of early Christianity was the challenge to express faith in more creative forms. When the one correct form was found, it was already past time to search for another. Theologians were always having to revise or rewrite. As Karl Barth worked and worked on his *Church Dogmatics*, he said that someone would have to begin another by the time he finished; then in creative fashion Barth abandoned his project in the realization that time had already outrun him. Valery was correct, "A poem is never finished; it is only abandoned."

Many have abandoned their copybook exercises in religion. Good for them. They are learning that life is lived *toward* answers, not *in* answers. "There is no definitive, timeless understanding which raises no more questions."[6] Answers are never answers; they are historical perspectives.

Religious folk have always been perplexed by this. We have that "changelessness" of God in our computers, that "ambassadors-of-the-truth" syndrome, that "Christ is the answer." As a child I probably saw too many Tarzan and Lone Ranger movies, probably read too many Superman comics, or, I heard too much *deus ex machina* in Sunday school. I was forever forgetting my trumpet, leaving it on the bus. Then almost home from the bus stop, the emptiness of one hand triggered an emptiness of the heart. I prayed fervently, believingly. The horn always turned up. It was God's doing; I was convinced of it. Now my Parent argues with my Child that the Almighty had more to do than chase off after buses as a favor to forgetful children.

[6]Eduard Schillebeeckx, *God The Future of Man* (New York: Sheed & Ward, 1968), p. 8.

I'd heard it somewhere. Perhaps it was the story of Joseph with the thread of God's providence woven through it. From the beginning of this story there is more than a hint that God has something special in mind for Joseph. He was destined. The account unfolds like an old Saturday movie serial. At the end of each installment, Joseph was caught in a sinister plot from which no one could possibly escape, but next Saturday, a miracle, snatched from the jaws of catastrophe again! Joseph's brothers plotted to kill him, but Reuben persuaded them to throw him into a pit where he would die of starvation. The writer adds, "The pit was empty, there was no water in it." Thank God for that! While the brothers ate, a caravan of merchants passed by on the way to Egypt. The brothers decided to sell Joseph as a slave. By the hundreds, slaves languished and died in Egypt, but not Joseph, "the Lord was with him," and he was made overseer in the house of Potiphar, captain of the guards. Potiphar's wife accused Joseph of improper advances; any other slave would have been killed on the spot. Not Joseph, "the Lord was with him," and he was thrown into prison. Then Joseph and the Lord went from dream to dream until he was second in command of all Egypt. Beautiful! And if for Joseph, why not for latter-day saints?

Or, was it that Daniel-in-the-lion's-den story

that gave me more promise than fulfillment? It was one of the first Bible stories I learned. Devoted Daniel would not worship idols; courageous Daniel would take his chances in the lion's den. An angel of the Lord stopped the mouths of those lions. Hurrah for the angel of the Lord! That story gets in the gut of little children; our side is way ahead.

All this I heard before I could read. The reading and thinking was my undoing. I read of post-biblical saints who chose lions' dens rather than sacrifice to idols. These saints had the Daniel story in *their* gut. The gates were opened, the lions loosed. They ripped those Christians, Daniel's kin, limb from limb. Had God gone out of the mouth-stopping business? God? Where *was* God? I have not understood God's providence for some time now. The facts of the case are obscure, and I am left with only the badge of my office. Robert Frost expressed my yearning to his star.

> Say something to us we can learn
> By heart and when alone repeat.
> Say something! And it says, "I burn."
> But say with what degree of heat.
> Talk Fahrenheit, talk Centigrade.
> Use language we can comprehend.[7]

[7]Take Something Like a Star," *The Poetry of Robert Frost,* ed. Edward Connery Lathem (New York: Holt, Rinehart and Winston, 1969), p. 403.

It is factual religion that I cherish—and that I also abhor.

This paradox threatens to prevent any religious wholeness, threatens to defeat the very purpose of religion: re-bind. Is there any glue durable enough to bind life together?

The first furniture I ever purchased were two unpainted captain's chairs. These Sears, Roebuck products, enhanced by my painter's skill, occupied the place of honor in our small kitchen. But after a few months, the chairs began to spread— rungs left legs; arms swayed. Everything about those chairs came unglued. I became a full-time agent of adhesives—gluing and gluing and gluing. Absolutely useless.

One day a wiry Czechoslovakian cabinet-maker visited in our home and sat in a wobbly chair that threatened to wrestle him to the ground, no holds barred. Novomesky asked for permission to take the chairs home with him to see if he could teach them better posture. In a week he was back with the same chairs, securely glued. I've never had to touch them since. "How did you do it?" I asked. He grinned, "An old trade secret. A Czechoslovakian mystery." For years now I have lived with that personal mystery of wholeness, experienced it without understanding it. It? Perhaps *God* is the word. Michael Novak sums it up: "Arrows of ritual, worship, dance, discourse are sent off into the dark. They fall short of pinning down precisely the one at whom they aim."[8] There are times, however, when I think I hear distinctly a yell of pain from that darkness, and it signifies a presence.

[8]Michael Novak, *Ascent of the Mountain, Flight of the Dove* (New York: Harper & Row, 1971), p. 76.

IV.
Religion: Help or Hindrance

Religion is a crutch! Every time I heard those lyrics they were set to a tune of derision. Human nature does not admire the crutch; it symbolizes dependence and weakness. But when you're crippled, a crutch can be a handy implement.

Religion is a crutch! Of course. Even those abandoned crutches dangling from the Basilica walls at Einsiedeln, Switzerland, tell only of physical cure; they were never intended to imply that their former owners would not need less tangible means of support. Men are deficient, cripples; religion helps them walk. It is a visible sign of our infirmity *and* the means of living with it. A crutch helps and hinders.

Robert Ingersoll's religious crutch kept tripping him. He caricatured a limping observance of the Sabbath. There was a sermon in which the preacher

> commenced at "first" and went on and on and on to about "twenty-thirdly." Then he made a few remarks by way of application; and then took a general view of the subject, and in about two hours reached the last chapter in Revelation.
>
> The morning service over, Sunday School set in. Then came the catechism with the chief end of man. . . . We sat in a row with our feet coming in about six inches of the floor. The minister asked us if we knew that we all deserved to go to hell, and we all answered "Yes." Then we were asked if we would be willing to go to hell if it was God's will, and every little liar shouted "Yes."

After Sunday school everybody had a quick lunch in order to allow a little time before the afternoon service so they could visit the graveyard and study epitaphs. The epitaphs, said Ingersoll, were "a great comfort. The reflection came to my mind that the observance of the Sabbath could not last always." [1] Ingersoll threw it all over, discarded his inherited crutch and went striding into a life devoid of all religion—so he said.

[1] Orvin Larson, *American Infidel: Robert G. Ingersoll* (New York: Citadel Press, 1962), p. 18.

History is strewn with abandoned crutches. We are not the first nor will we be the last to see persons turn from religion. I am sympathetic with those who find other than religious crutches. Already, I have confessed the preference to crawl rather than be supported by a religion that discourages me from the development of my own muscles, a religion that would keep one in an infant's stroller all one's life. I remember the pathetic case of some small children who were to "perform" before a religious gathering. Each child was given his orthodox answer to memorize. He did not know what the question would be; he only knew that when the leader asked something and looked at him, he was to give his answer. It was the teacher's responsibility to ask the correct question. There was a rehearsal to eliminate the possibility of any error. It was a foolproof scheme. On the night of the performance, however, the teacher lapsed more and more into spontaneity; perhaps it was the limelight, and then, too, this program had gone so well to this point. She would, she said, ask each boy to introduce himself before the religious examination began. She looked at the first boy in line and asked, "What is your name, son?" "Cooperative program," came the reply. "No, no," said the flustered teacher, "just tell us your name first." Two more times the boy gave his memorized answer—"Cooperative

72

program." It was the correct answer to some question. A few years later that boy threw away his religious crutch. Good riddance.

This is a time of frantic cleaning in the religious temples of the world. Crutches are being discarded with the naïve abandon of the "healed" in some tawdry faith-healer's tent; the inevitable stumbling and falling is everywhere.

Religionless Christianity is what the world—and the church—need, declared Dietrich Bonhoeffer. Karl Barth has a section in his *Church Dogmatics* titled "The Revelation of God as the Abolition of Religion." This emphasis led to the needed reform of religion, the renewal of churches, and, not a little premature, abandonment of all crutches.

It was actually religion that first caught my attention, told me of God, of myself, and offered me a sense of mission. Religion told me all this—and faith made it believable. Perhaps it was God using religious forms; the professional said it was. Perhaps God had to hack his way through the forms to reach me and I heard him in spite of all the religious talk. I don't know, but at some point I was invited to join; "called" is the religious word. A good word, one used by those early Christians to describe their company, "called-out ones." Those "called" of the Lord.

A young man stayed away from worship for

several weeks after he had preached his first sermon before his home church. When the pastor bumped into him one day, he rebuked him for his absence and reminded him of his statement that he felt the Lord had called him to preach. "I did think so," whined the young man, "but after the Lord heard me try, I think he gave up the idea."

For ten years as a professor of theology, I watched them come and go—those professionally called of the Lord. There was an arrogance in some of them, born of naïveté; an authority in some, born of devotion and self-sacrifice; an ignorance in some, born of sloth; a hope in most, born of belief. They were the Lord's own. Called from butcher shops and office desks and college classrooms. Called by mothers and grandmothers and fathers and heroes, and by God. There were others called by draft deferments and by sincere search for meaning and by a desire to serve their fellowmen. All of them called—in one way or another. Some of the best were least certain of that "call," and some of the worst had no doubts at all. I remember one of the latter who spoke glowingly and piously, oh so piously, of his gratitude to God at being "called" to attend classes at the seminary. Three weeks later God had "called" him to be pastor of a church in south Georgia. Shame on that fickle-minded God and his capricious calls.

The church made a serious mistake when "the

called" were unionized and ministry became a closed shop. Now the clergy receive engraved "calls" addressed to them personally; the laity get mimeographed circulars addressed "Occupant." Clergy are called; laity decide. In Western religions this "mistake" is well on the way toward correction.

It is religion that hands one the phone and says, "Someone wants to speak with you." Then, by faith, I hear *my* name called. I realize my addressability. I am known outside my self-knowledge; I exist in the person of another. Watch small children choosing sides for some game: two captains are selected by mutual consent who choose alternately until all the candidates are exhausted. In every group there is at least one child who knows that he will not be first choice or second or fifth. He only wants to be chosen. He can live with the position. But to see the choosing go against you, to hear one of the captains say, "O.K. You take Joe. We don't want him anyway." Choosing can be rough on the ego.

There is good news in Dag Hammarskjöld's words: "The way chose you—And you must be thankful." And that statement of Jesus': "I have chosen you." And Paul's notion that faith has turned nobodies into somebodies.

Religion mediates such a call, and the call itself enables the one addressed to respond. It is more than decision, more than resolution of the will. It is a gift, the gift of response: God-within-us responding to God-without-us.

Mother Teresa, the Yugoslavian nun who went to India to help the poor and the dying, said of her order:

> We must be able to radiate the joy of Christ, express it in our actions. If our actions are just useful actions that give no joy to the people, our poor people would never be able to rise up to the call which we want them to hear, the call to come closer to God. We want to make them feel that they are loved.[2]

I am addressed, therefore, I am, and love is at least a state of attention.

The land was famished for "the word of the Lord" when young Samuel dozed in the temple and "the lamp of God had not yet gone out." A call slipped into the boy's ears, vibrated in his head, and his brains sent his legs running off to the only caller he knew to be close at hand. "No," said the old priest Eli, "I did not call." There it was again and again, his very own name. But if not Eli, then who? "God," answered the priest. "Listen to the call of God."

Dozing in a temple of conservative orthodoxy,

[2]Malcolm Muggeridge, *Something Beautiful for God* (New York: Harper & Row, 1971), p. 98.

the religion embodied in a community of worshipers named my caller for me, wrote his name
on rickety blackboards, pointed to it on brightly
colored Sunday school cards. Religious persons
asked me to repeat what I had heard the way a
two- or three-year-old child identifies animals in a
picture book. The pictures of God, however, were
in such poor focus; they kept disappearing from
view just when I thought I was visualizing the
features. "God is not an old grandfatherly type,
sitting in a rocking chair somewhere in the sky."
What a disappointment! I had loved and admired
both my grandfathers. Oh, I don't think I ever
imagined that God resembled either, but this
negative revelation caused me to "see" God as less
than grandfatherly for a few years. It was the pain
of absence. The same pain I felt when Santa Claus
was demythologized by a slightly older relative.

Rudolf Bultmann claimed that *"a new image of
God"* was necessary for post-Copernican man since
the old ecclesiastical one was obsolete. I suppose
each generation in its struggle for humanity labors
with an image of God. At least I have seen that in
persons for whom religion was a raging fever. God
is in the hands of angry sinners, always, and only
the religious know themselves as sinners. Only the
religious know how little they truly believe.

Men have expressed a preference for an omnipotent, omniscient, omnipresent deity. W. H. Auden

has King Herod challenge the incarnationists by asking:

"Why can't people be sensible? . . . Why can't they see that the notion of a finite God is absurd?"[3]

Is that the reason the Gospels of Matthew and Luke undermine incarnation with their theory of virgin birth? Is that why other biblical characters wanted as much space as possible between "the Christ" and "suffering"? Messiah must not, could not suffer, they argued until they were red in the face.

Religious men and women have dedicated themselves to the protection of divine security. They have crusaded to rescue the deity from the hands of the heathen. They have been solicitous lest their God dash his foot against a modern concept. "My God can beat your God." "God can do anything." If God is omnipotent, why all the bodyguards?

There is at the same time, an underside to our religious desires that is repulsed by divine omnipotence. We resent an all-powerful, all-knowing God the way we resent a wife or a friend who is always right about everything. Who dares live with such a constant reminder of one's own

[3]W. H. Auden, "For the Time Being," *Collected Longer Poems*, (New York Random House, 1969), p. 189.

weakness? Nietzsche spoke for the underdogs when he wrote:

> He looked with eyes which beheld *everything,*—he beheld men's depths and dregs, all his hidden ignominy and ugliness. His pity knew no modesty: he crept into my dirtiest corners. This most prying, over-intrusive, over-pitiful one had to die. . . .
> The God who beheld everything, *and also man:* that God had to die! Man cannot *endure* it that such a witness should live.[4]

Man yearns *for* yet strives *against* the Absolute. He is deeply embarrassed by his inability to comprehend completely, to act absolutely. Must God's power be purchased at the price of man's pride? Why not a less powerful God for the sake of a more powerful man—God becoming man, "taking his own medicine" as Georgia Harkness said, sharing man's weakness? There is a biblical thesis that God is never stronger, never more godlike, than in his self-accepted weakness.

The Christian finds salvation in a powerful God who suffers: "body broken for you; blood shed for you." In Jesus, God is always giving himself into the hands of men. Paul Scherer said, "If Jesus means anything, there are tears in God's eyes." This is all human talk of God, a weak pointing, but

[4]Friedrich Nietzsche, *Thus Spake Zarathustra* (New York: Modern Library), p. 297.

then we humans *are* weak pointers. There is no other way, and in Jesus we have God's blessing on the weakness of pointing. Marc Connelly had it expressed on the stage for all to see and hear, "Even bein' Gawd ain't a bed of roses." Oh, there's joy and humor and fish fries and ten-cent cigars at the opening of *The Green Pastures*, but before it's over God is in for one hard time. As the play closes, the Almighty God ponders a conversation with Hezdrel about learning mercy through suffering.

God asks: "Did he mean dat even God must suffer?"

Then a voice is heard offstage: "Oh, look at him! Oh, look, dey goin' to make him carry it up dat high hill! Dey goin' to nail him to it! Oh, dat's a terrible burden for one man to carry!"

God rises and murmurs: "Yes!"

Then all the angels burst into singing: "Hallelujah, King Jesus," as the lights begin to fade.[5]

This was "the Way," *Via Dolorosa.* I saw it in Cecil B. DeMille's "King of Kings"; I heard of it in John Bunyan's *Pilgrim's Progress.* Almost every Sunday of my childhood, religious teachers and preachers spoke of Christianity as "the way of life." They believed it, lived it more and less.

Religions of all stripes have enabled devotees to

[5]Marc Connelly, *The Green Pastures,* (New York: Rinehart & Company, Inc., 1959), pp. 172-173.

celebrate life as movement, as way. The religious "rites of passage" were poles passing by our windows—proof of motion: presentation, baptism, confirmation, marriage, death. Sacraments of pilgrimage. Purposive passage into the future.

One does not choose to live toward the future; if he or she lives she moves into the future, *unless,* she chooses to live in the past. And even then she cannot actually live there, she can only remember that she has lived. Most persons lack the courage or despair to commit suicide in an absolute manner; they compromise by leaving a part of themselves behind. The historical landscape is strewn with bits and pieces of themselves while they move reluctantly, piecemeal into the future. How long can we leave pieces behind before we are present nobodies, our real selves elsewhere? Remember those boring afternoons reliving the past with someone who refused to face the present and the future?

How can we discard our past? That was the question facing the Joad family in Steinbeck's *The Grapes of Wrath.* Only the bare necessities could be taken to California. There simply wasn't room, but how do you decide what parts of the past to leave?

And the children came.
If Mary takes that doll, that dirty rag doll, I got to take my Injun bow. I got to. An' this roun'

stick—big as me. I might need this stick. I had this
stick so long—a month, or maybe a year. I got to
take it. . . .

The women sat among the doomed things . . .
This book. My father had it. He liked a book.
Pilgrim's Progress. Used to read it. Got his name in
it. And his pipe—still smells rank. And this
picture—an angel. I looked at that before the fust
three come—didn't seem to do much good. Think
we could get this china dog in? Aunt Sadie brought
it from the St. Louis Fair. See? Wrote right on it.
No, I guess not. Here's a letter my brother wrote
the day before he died. Here's an old-time hat.
These feathers—never got to use them. No, there
isn't room.

How can we live without our lives? How will we
know it's us without our past? No. Leave it.[6]

The past is conserved in religious forms. Men have
lived and worshiped before us, have pointed to
the activity of God in their midst, have hoped in
the future—our present. It was tradition, says
Tevye, that enabled the Jews of Anatevka to
maintain their precarious balance while fiddling
on the roof. It was tradition that caused each
inhabitant to know who he was and what God
expected him to do. The past lives for all of us in
our memory and in our imagination and in our
thanksgiving and in our tradition.

[6]John Steinbeck, *The Grapes of Wrath*. (New York: Viking Press,
1966), p. 120.

Of course the past can be preserved in rigid, cracked forms; of course religious persons can see themselves as custodians of the sacred archives.

> I'm afraid there's many a spectacled sod
> Prefers the British Museum to God.[7]

And while Auden's couplet was probably written with another point in mind, substitute "religious" for "British" and you'll be face to face with many of the devout. But religion must not be evaluated by its failures anymore than by any other style of life.

"Christianity," proclaimed Karl Rahner, "is the religion of the absolute future." "Faith," wrote Gerhard Ebeling, "is openness to the future." "The kingdom of heaven," according to Jesus, "is like a grain of mustard seed" with big plans germinating in its tiny form. What a mouthful of hope there is in all these sayings.

Religion mediates a *hope*ful future: the exiled author of Second Isaiah, standing knee deep in shattered dreams, crying aloud, "Remember not the former things, nor consider the things of old. Behold, [God is] doing a new thing", (43:18-19). Religious hope is a young Galilean peasant girl with a bellyful of God singing the Magnificat; it's a bawling babe in a manger surrounded by

[7] W. H. Auden, "Shorts," *Collected Shorter Poems,* (N. Y.: Random House, 1966), p. 42.

heavenly hosts and men who dared to tell the story as truth; it's a tanned carpenter turned teacher using a smelly fishing boat as a classroom, speaking of the abundant life; it's a sagging, spent man on a cross with a sign fluttering in the wind—King of the Jews; it's that ever-present declaration "Christ the Lord is risen *today*."

Hope mediated through religious forms has a certain illogical character, an unbelievableness. It, as faith, is not conjured up; it is gift. One is called to hope, released to hope, as though the light of hope needed a black backdrop to make it visible. Resurrection out of death. A soon-to-be-killed black dreamer shouting out that dream. A remnant. A mustard seed. Father Daniel Berrigan voiced the naïve, adolescent character of hope in a poem titled "Laurel."

They had 280 languages
and 4,862 local dialects
in which to say
no hope   no future   not a chance

when they invaded the interior
they brought along
a few phrases in pidgin
no hope   no future   not a chance

the savages laid aside
their feathers, beads, masks

and the gods whose painted images
adorned the moving boat

nevertheless
here and there in the dust
where man may touch the living green

I spell
like a finger
across blind deaf flesh
HOPE   FUTURE   CHANCE [8]

Christianity has always had in its quiver the arrow of hope to be shot into the future—a "nevertheless" pinning despair to some tree of life. Recall once more the despair of a small child who fears that he will not be chosen for the team, and stand that image beside one furnished by Harry Emerson Fosdick who told of a boy coming home from school one day with the proud announcement, "I am the assistant to the assistant manager of the third football team." There's a tiny mustard seed of hope for you.

After reading Steinbeck's *The Grapes of Wrath*, I was depressed for days. The characters are familiar to me—cousins, aunts, uncles, friends. As I read I kept projecting better days for the Joads, but their life goes from bad to worse and ends in absolute

[8] Daniel Berrigan, *False Gods, Real Men* (Toronto: The Macmillan Co., 1969), p. 89.

futility and despair. No, not quite *absolute* futility. There is a slight ray of hope. When the family are forced to leave their farm and travel to California, the young daughter, Rose of Sharon, has just become pregnant. They move from job to job, from little food to no food, from a united family to a remnant. There is a growing anxiety that Rose of Sharon's unborn baby is not receiving the amount or the type nourishment it needs; yet, nothing can be done. The baby is born dead. Then, in a rush, the story ends in a flooded boxcar that has to be abandoned along with their remaining posses- sions. The struggling remnant of a family seeks shelter from the rain in an old barn. There, on the last page of the novel, they discover a starving man and his son. The little boy pleads for help for his father, and in embarrassed self-denial, hope is reborn as Rose of Sharon feeds the starving man from her swollen breasts.

Life is movement-in-time—an hour, a day, a week, a month, a year, an unfolding—the creases still visible. At some new unfoldings there is less adherence to past forms; persons seem more willing to spill over the bank, take fewer precau- tions. A new era dawned when the ships no longer hugged the coasts but spread over the oceans, said Bertolt Brecht. There are signs that we have come into such an "open situation," with the entire world coming to focus "here and now" upon the individual, "offering him the conditions of his action." The old order has less hold on men and women. They are, declared Dietrich von Oppen, no longer bound to "preformed situations with preformed answers."[9]

Brecht depicted the strains of entering a new order in his play *Galileo*. Clouds of censure and rejection surrounded the scientist from the very beginning. Galileo believed that the telescope would free men from slavery to the old order; they must believe what they see. Yet, the scholars refused to view the heavens through this man-made tube. All truth concerning the universe had already been discovered and certified. Whereupon Galileo quoted, "Truth is the daughter of Time, not of Authority."[10]

[9]See Dietrich von Oppen, "Man in the Open Situation,"*Journal for Theology and the Church,* vol. 2, *Translating Theology into the Modern Age* (New York: Harper & Row, 1965).
[10]Bertolt Brecht, *Galileo.* (New York: Grove Press, 1966), p. 68.

V.
Religion: Substance or Shadow

What a catalog of humanity the Bible is. Dress it all we like in somber or brightly colored leather from Morocco, gilt edges, with "Holy" stamped in letters six inches tall, but its humanity cannot be disguised. That hangs out in Jacob and David, Peter and Judas, Barnabas and Paul.

Things fell so neatly into place when Barnabas and Paul and John Mark entered the ministry. Simple laymen, who have always had difficulty knowing what terms to apply to clergymen and their sermons, smiled and said of these three musketeers, "They're going places." And they were. "In the power of the Spirit," they sailed for Cyprus where victory followed victory until even the governor became a convert. Leaving Cyprus they sailed to Perga. "John Mark, however, left them and returned to Jerusalem"—one of the first of a long line of clerical dropouts.

This resignation implied a permanency for Paul that was not true for Barnabas; therefore, when the two were ready to leave on their second missionary journey, Barnabas had Mark in tow once more. "No," declared Paul adamantly. "Not this time." Perhaps he quoted those words about putting your hand to the plow and looking back, thereby disqualifying yourself. Whatever the arguments, there was a sharp dispute; hot, angry words were spoken. Faith, hope, and love could not hold it all together. Paul left in a huff, taking only Silas with him. Mark tagged along with Barnabas.

John Mark was no Paul and he knew it. He was in sandals too large for his feet, but he was being loved to size. Religion, the cause of his most shameful embarrassment, was forming a salvation for him, and someday he would write it all down.

How long did it take Mark to live down that nagging desertion? How long before he could believe that Barnabas loved rather than pitied him? No way to tell, but I surmise that it took *him* longer than anyone else. It always does. We are harder on ourselves than others could possibly be.

We dig up the bones of past failures and use them in a constant ritual of self-flagellation. Uncle John of Steinbeck's *Grapes of Wrath* could never forgive himself for allowing his pregnant young wife to die of a ruptured appendix. At the time he was sure that it was only a bellyache. All the trailing years had been filled with attempts to relieve his guilt, the search for self-forgiveness. Tom describes his uncle:

> He's all the time makin' it up to somebody—givin' kids stuff, droppin' a sack a meal on somebody's porch. Give away about ever'thing he got, an' still he ain't very happy.
> He'd come to our house in the night sometimes, an' we knowed he come 'cause jus' as sure as he come there'd be a pack a gum in the bed right beside ever' one of us. We thought he was Jesus Christ Awmighty.[1]

Innocent until proved guilty? Tell that to Uncle John or try convincing yourself.

We live in the fear that our past will catch up with us, will walk into a room one night and right there before all our friends and loved ones cry, "I know this man." Or, our present impotence will be discovered. "Drop your pants," the doctor will say, and there before God and everyone we will be

[1] John Steinbeck, *The Grapes of Wrath* (New York: Viking Press, 1966), pp. 92-93.

known. It is not that the past or the present is so sordid; we might even boast of that in Hemingway fashion. The past and present are filled to the brim with inadequacies—all the times and places that we didn't measure up, the AWOLs of our lives. Isn't that the reason we stay on the run, fill our schedules with more than we can possibly do, to avoid "quiet times"? We try to escape ourselves, run away from the self. Man's paradox is this: he cannot stand the sight of the one he loves most of all.

Due to this personal estimation of the self, it is next to impossible to believe that anyone else could care for us—and if they did we couldn't respect them. We refuse to believe that we are lovable. Why else do we bathe incessantly and swab on deodorants and use toothpaste that will keep our breaths fresh for hours? Why do we grin and nod and shift and go through a little ritual every time we meet a stranger? Why must we be the life of *every* party?

We have the distinct impression that we are out of shape—grown flabby physically, morally, spiritually. A rigid program of calisthenics has availed us nothing. Nor have the high-powered public relations firms convinced many—even the secretary of defense must doubt his nationalism at times.

In *The Trial*, Kafka's Joseph K. wanders about

in a vain attempt to discover the charge against him, to find one person who can or will tell him what wrong he has done, one person who will believe in him. The "crime" is incompleteness, says Paul, a falling short of the glory of God, estrangement from the Ground of Being, a clod broken off from the main, the crime of humanity, the high price paid for our ability to discern.

That ancient religious myth of beginnings displays clearly the price tag of perspicacity. Man was not to eat the fruit on the tree in the center of the garden, for it was the elixir of discernment. The installments on this purchase would last a lifetime—and more. Yet, the fruit was eaten, eyes were opened. Man knew that he was naked, knew the presence of evil in the world, knew the widening gulf between himself and his Creator, and, worst of all, knew that he did not know.

Archibald MacLeish peers into the hell of discernment in the prologue of his play *J. B.* Mr. Zuss plays the part of God while Nickles wears the Satanmask. The lights fade out; the dialogue begins, and from behind the Satanmask comes a snicker and then a loud guffaw. Mr. Zuss tears his mask off and rebukes Nickles for laughing. Nickles responds:

> Do I look as though I'd laughed?
> If you had seen what I have seen

You'd never laugh again! . . .

> Weep either . . .

Those eyes *see*. (Nickles points to the Satanmask)

They see the *world*. They do. They see it.
From going to and fro in the earth,
From walking up and down, they see it.
I know what Hell is now—to *see*.
Consciousness of consciousness . . .[2]

The Christian religion holds this myth of "fall"
before my face. I recognize myself, see my
imperfection, my incompleteness, know that
something of selfhood has been left behind,
somewhere. The "good man" is a walking ghost,
kept alive by the piosity of positive thinking and
shallow optimism. The "good man" is a recurring
illusion propagated by the blind who suppress
their ability to discern. This illusion, said Jung,
"befogged people's minds when they were no
longer able to understand the dogma of original
sin. . . ."[3] Nietzsche felled the "good man," and
Freud buried the corpse, and if any survived this
slaughter, the barbarism of the twentieth century
should have taken care of them.

[2]Archibald MacLeish, *J. B.* (Boston: Houghton Mifflin, 1958), pp. 21-22.
[3]C. G. Jung, *Psychological Reflections* (New York: Harper & Row, 1961), p. 245.

So, where is the Good? For weeks I studied the dialogues of Plato. There was much talk of "the Good," but I was far more interested in correct translation, the proper tenses of Greek verbs, the meaning of Greek idioms. I was to be tested on the translation not the understanding. Now, I have forgotten the identity of "the Good."

"Good Master, what must I do to have eternal life?" "Don't call me 'Good,'" says the teacher. "Only God is Good." Of course: "God is good. God is great." But that was so long ago, so far away, and I forget where it was supposed to lead. I can only recall, in the foggiest sort of way, that I lost something there, somewhere in the past, and again this morning. It was, I think, the innocence of invincibility. And what makes me so sad? I should have known.

Southerners above all Americans should know innately this loss of innocence, sacrificed to a sociological exploitation of blacks. We were bribed, bought off, in our grandfathers and great grandfathers, by the large, powerful landowners with their black possessions.

It was not always that way. The religion that told us who we were also held up a better way. In 1789 the Baptist General Committee of Virginia adopted the following statement:

Resolved, That slavery is a violent deprivation of the rights of nature and inconsistent with a

republic government, and therefore recommend it
to our brethren to make use of every legal measure
to extirpate this horrid evil from the land. . . .

By 1837, however, there was not a single anti-
slavery society in the South, and regional loyalty
was evaluated in terms of conformity of thought
on this peculiar institution. The fallen were falling.
The South turned in on itself, resisted and
resented all "outside" interference with its way of
life, and developed a guilt-feeling compounded by
an inferiority complex that persists to this day.
Lost innocence is never recoverable.

There is a story recorded only by Luke that
illustrates the point I wish to make. It's the story of
a man searching for the pieces of himself. Interest-
ingly enough they began to appear and to fit when
he heard his name on someone else's lips.
"Zacchaeus," called Jesus, "make haste and come
down; for I must stay at your house today." As
they dined together, there was the usual strained
conversation between strangers about the
weather—"We haven't had rain in Jericho for two
months now, Rabbi," about vocations—"How's
the fishing on Lake Gennesaret?" about travels—
"I passed through Galilee a month ago. No, it was
longer. Let's see, must have been a month and a
half. Anyway, I hardly recognized the section with
all the new building going on." It was the

uncomfortable conversation of a knowledgeable man, the pretense of one who reeked of exploitation. It was the rambling search for something to say that would justify one's existence: "I am even more than a name." Suddenly Zacchaeus stood and blurted out loudly, "Rabbi, half my goods I give to the poor." Careful, Zacchaeus, watch yourself, keep your mouth under control or you'll have one honey of a hangover tomorrow. But the Little Big Man went on, "And if I have defrauded anyone, I will restore it fourfold." "My God," thought the servants, "he has lost his mind. He wants to buy back his innocence." As Zacchaeus sank back on his couch he heard the Rabbi say, "Today, salvation has come to this house." It was *metanoia*, "change of direction"—repentance.

There is a sadness that leads to death and a sadness that leads to life. The joy of repentance is realized only in the latter way. The sadness unto death is a form of religious remorse that usually issues in negative moralism. Such calls to repentance almost always have a faulty biblical base. A hundred years ago a Baptist preacher in Kentucky said, "Of all the pastimes in vogue, none is so captivating, so bewitching, as the dance— especially to young females; and no serpent of the coil diffuses a more deadly venom." Even the dancing mentioned in the Bible could not be approved according to this Kentucky Baptist, for

"the dancing of Herodia's daughter before Herod
. . . cost the life of the first Baptist the world ever
saw."[4]

All over the South this sadness unto death has
left its lingering stench. There has been remorse,
but our sorrow has not led to repentance. We have
wallowed in our grief, pitied ourselves and others,
filled steaming revival tents and air-conditioned
sanctuaries. In our not-so-veiled boasts about the
improvements in race relations, there has been
little or no genuine willingness to repent. Even the
minuscule amount of repentance has been
drowned out by the dragging of so many heels. We
have denied ourselves the joy of repentance—and
we are not alone!

The prophet Joel pegged it correctly: there has
been a rending of garments rather than a tearing of
hearts. The *rites* of repentance have superseded the
rights. We are a sad people.

Americans have looked long into the depths of
despair and more than partly believed what was
seen. We watched all the funerals on television—
even some of the assassinations. We were sad and
depressed for days, wept for what might have
been. We dragged around our guilt and shame,
dragged it laboriously, carefully, tenderly, and we
searched for our lost innocence. When President

[4]W. C. Buck, "Games and Dancing," *Southern Baptist Review &
Eclectic* (July 1857).

John F. Kennedy was slain, we went to a Roman Catholic Mass for the first time and felt better for a short period. When Dr. Martin Luther King, Jr., was felled, we smiled sympathetically at all the black faces we saw, reached out and touched hands, and felt better for a short period. But we did not repent. We shared a common sadness, but it was a sadness that leads to death. We longed for joy, still do, but not at the price of repentance.

Why, for God's sake, did Israel allow her disobedience, infidelity, inadequacy, imperfection to be spread all over the pages of her holy book? For God's sake! "Don't forget who brought us out of slavery," remind the writers. "Don't forget who sustained us in the desert"; "don't forget God's faithfulness reaching through our unfaithfulness"; "don't forget . . ." It's all there in the Bible, but since we have kept company with translators rather than interpreters, we shelved that book. Was it irrelevance, or did we give it up because we did not like what we read and heard, because we lacked the courage to stand under the Word?

According to the biblical word, man is sinner, not in and of himself, but *before God*. Without this stance-before-God, man can believe in his own goodness, can imagine a human adequacy that makes God superfluous. Thomas Merton had this in mind when he wrote of some who "have tasted the sickness that is present in the inmost heart of man estranged from his God by guilt, suspicion and covert hatred. If that sickness is an illusion, then there is no need for the Cross, the sacraments and the Church."[5] Cross, sacraments, and church—vital forms of the Christian religion; promissory notes signed by God.

The writer of the First Letter of John worded it and that English King had the best translator: "Now are we the children of God." *"Now"*—note redeemed, cash in the pocket even as we begin the journey. Too much has been said about men who saw mirrored in the eyes of Jesus the persons they could become. *"Now* are we the children of God." And we can hardly imagine what we shall become. But, *now.* In this recognition we are freed to be who we are. In this *faith*ful recognition, we surrender the option of nonbeing. We *are.* Listen: "in him [God] we live and move and *have* our being."

It is the reality of an authentic existence, playing the cards that have been dealt. Henrik Ibsen wrote a verse play titled *Brand* in which the main character, an uncompromising pastor with a stern theology, reaches a modicum of mature acceptance of life by the second act. It takes most of us at least that long. Brand declares:

[5] Thomas Merton, *Contemplative Prayer* (New York: B. Herder Book Co., 1969), p. 134.

This morning visions flocked to me
Like wild swans, and lifted me on their broad
wings.
I looked outwards, thinking my path lay there.
I saw myself as the chastiser of the age,
Striding in greatness above the tumult.
The pomp of processions, hymns
And incense, silken banners, golden cups,
Songs of victory, the acclaim
Of surging crowds, glorified my life's work.
But it was an empty dream, a mountain mirage
Made by the sun in the morning mist.
Now I stand in a deep valley, where darkness
Falls long before evening. I stand between
The mountain and the sea, far from the tumult
Of the world. But this is my home.
My Sunday song is over, my winged steed
Can be unsaddled. My duty lies here.
There is a higher purpose than the glory of
battle:
To hallow daily toil to the praise of God.[6]

In some religious book I kept reading that I was
all right—righteous. The war between the Self and
my self was over if I could believe, trust, and obey.
Perhaps they were singing "Just As I Am" the
night I "went forward" to affirm what was already
happening. Whether the believers sang it then or
not, I don't know, but we sang it so often that I still

[6]Henrik Ibsen, *Brand* (Garden City, N.Y.: Anchor Books, Double-day & Company, Inc., 1960), pp. 85-86.

have it tucked away in my gut. I shall always be grateful for that. For a long time I hid that gratitude and repressed the old gospel hymn, only to have it slip out of that repression and appear in a hum or a whistle when my guard was down. One day I read a sermon James Pike had preached when he was dean of the Cathedral of St. John the Divine, a sermon based on that same old gospel hymn. Good reformed theology, concluded Pike. And it is!

By God, I can live with my self, accept all the inadequacies and failures. By God, I can unsaddle my winged steed. I can be man-before-God and man-before-my-neighbor. For that I am thankful. On some days I really do believe God, lean on him, know that I am a word uttered by God, "containing a partial thought of Himself."

Believers are *some* bodies, the essence of reality. They cast shadows. Isn't that what the historian says in the fifth chapter of Acts? "They even carried out the sick into the streets, and laid them on beds and pallets, that as Peter came by at least his shadow might fall on some of them" (5:15).

I cast a shadow, therefore I am. Not exactly Descartes, but at least an analogy that points in the right direction.

Not only does my shadow bear silent testimony to my existence, it is mission. To be and to do, with the conjunction becoming thinner and thinner until being and doing merge—a word spoken by God. No one need strive to make a shadow. Only substance and light are needed.

One of the finest tributes ever paid any teacher was written of a professor at Columbia University:

> Mark the tiger
>   prowled the
> ways of the world
> and we prowled
> with him
>
> Mark turned the world
>   to the light
> quietly and wonderingly:
>   we saw the lights
>   and colors
>   shooting through it
>
> he stood in front of
>   every tree and stone
>   and gourd and vine
> amazed at the wonder
> of their being
>
> we stood too
>   amazed at trees and vines,
>   amazed at him
>
> Mark is a poet
> and a teacher too,
> a teacher and a learner:
> he learns as trees get green
>   from sunlight

he teaches as a tree
gives shade. . . .[7]

Precisely. He is and he teaches—one and the same. He does not have a vocation; he is one. Substance, shadow.

It was a sun day, the type day to cast shadows though that had not really been our intention. We had gathered to worship, to have "the gutters of our minds cleaned." We had been all through the proper religious forms—bowed, sang, prayed, preached, departed. I was walking back down the nave when I saw a handwritten card propped against a column; it read: "A church makes you feel like you're the only person who is really living. It makes you feel a little bit more worthwhile when you walk out. For this the word thank you will have to suffice." For at least someone that Sunday, religion had provided a form with substance.

Whoever we are, we are to others. Religion did not begin with us, and it will not stop there, probably will not even slow down there. The Hebrews had no word for *destiny*. They had a covenant: You will be my people and I will be your God. That's all, but it has been stretching religious people ever since.

[7]Elizabeth D. Dodds, compiler, *Voices of Protest & Hope* (New York: Friendship Press, 1965), p. 157.

In his novel *Go Tell It on the Mountain,* James Baldwin gives a vignette on mission with covenant. John's father, writes Baldwin,

> was only a caretaker in the house of God. He was responsible for the replacement of burnt out light bulbs, and for the cleanliness of the church, and the care of the Bibles, and the hymn-books, and the placards on the walls. On Friday night he conducted the Young Ministers' Service and preached with them. Rarely did he bring the message on a Sunday morning; only if there was no one else to speak was his father called upon. He was a kind of fill-in speaker, a holy handyman.[8]

Church is a retinue of "holy handymen," working different shifts, for different pay, with different abilities, but the same mission.

Tenting at the base of Mt. Sinai, hearing that they were God's people, a holy nation with a lengthening shadow, Israel was born. There on the hot desert sands God ordained an entire nation of priests. Without the discipline of academic accomplishment, with no ecclesiastical garb to wear, these people were given holy orders.

It was a frank admission on God's part that the world needed caretakers, that he needed missioners. With boldness Meister Eckhart wrote, "God

[8]James Baldwin, *Go Tell It on the Mountain* (New York: Dell Books, 1965), pp. 50-51.

can as little do without us, as we without him." The expendability of man makes for sound orthodoxy, but God has often been more practical than orthodox.

Israel, old and new, was/is a kingdom of priests. There were special priests, Levites, clergy, bishops, but each citizen of the kingdom knows some worth in the ministry he performs for another. How lonely life would be waiting for the professional to make his rounds. What in heaven's name would church be if only the professionals could mediate between man and God? It would be a lie, and millions who have been served by a priestly neighbor would have to call it that. A denominational form requested: "How many ministers are there in your congregation?" How the statistics must have been warped when we wrote the figure "1600" in that space. In naming ministers we cannot possibly stop after listing Moses and Aaron and a successive line of touched clergy. How could I omit the name of that holy handywoman who boosted me up one week so that I could see a little future over the wall of that dead-end street I was on?

For too long religious persons have given most of their attention to the conversion of verbs into nouns. We have concentrated on "freedom" and ignored "freeing." We have researched "faith" but avoided "faithing." Christians have debated "ministry" but have not "ministered." To be a minister is not so much to occupy an office as it is to have a function.

The verbs are the trouble. Try learning a foreign language. Remember? The verbs, transitive and intransitive, active and passive; the verbs, controlling the endings on nouns, dragging nouns into action, giving life to the whole. Nouns test your memory, your vocabulary skill; verbs test your endurance, your sanity.

Holy handymen, arise. The future belongs to you. For two decades now the church has been turning in your direction. It is the hour of your *raison d'être*.

Church *is* a charismatic community—a group of persons who live by the gifts they bring to one another. Church is gifted people, not in some cerebral advantage but in an essential way. Church is graceful, not necessarily as a pirouetting ballerina, but as a body well fitted together and full of *charisma*. "Free gift," that's what *charisma* means. Gift, to and from, flowing freely, rising and ebbing, coming and going. The gift may come to you but it cannot, will not stop at you.

> Who died in Nineteen-Sixty-Five
> more worthy of honors
>   than *Lark*, a cow
> who gave to mankind

one-hundred-and-fifteen-thousand
litres of milk?[9]

Which goes to show that Auden knew his
charisma. Lark possessed a gift to be given. "I'll do
my best," says a devoutly religious soul. No.
Rather, share your gift, pool your resources, build
up the Body. If not a Lark then some other
cow—perhaps even man or woman.

We were standing beside the campus flagpole
when I asked my small friend, "What do you want
to be when you grow up?" Without hesitation he
replied, "A man." Of course. What else? And that
is not as easy as we have supposed. Then came the
shocker, the boy turned his face up to mine and
asked, "What do *you* want to be when *you* grow
up?" Is my immaturity all that evident, I wondered. Inadequacies hanging out for all to see? No,
it was innocence handing me a future. There
beside the flagpole the professor had found a
master teacher, and he grew in stature and in favor
with God and man—and self.

The apostle Paul knew life from both sides. He
adopted a rigorous program of self-improvement,
kept all the training rules religiously, ate only
approved food. He was determined to be first
team. One day, right in the midst of a weight

[9]W. H. Auden, *City Without Walls and Other Poems* (New York:
Random House, 1969), p. 61.

107

press, he allowed the weights to crash to the floor, picked up a piece of chalk and wrote across the blackboard, "Garbage!" (see Philippians 3:8). Once outside the gymnasium the muscle-bound rabbi was captivated by a band of Gypsies. Traveling in their company he experienced dancing and singing and rejection and suspicion. One day in this pilgrimage family, he announced, "By the grace of God I am what I am." They celebrated almost the entire night to welcome him home.

"It wasn't that way at all," protests Orthodoxy. "There was a vision, a judgment, prayers, repentance, and dedication to discipleship." That is precisely what I said; only the words were changed to indict the innocent.

A program of self-improvement was exchanged for one of self-acceptance. Something happens *in* you. Someone happens *to* you. You recognize yourself as a gift of God. There are also vibrations from some other that enable you to live more comfortably with yourself. Someone recognizes the substance of your gift.

An elderly patient in a frayed bathrobe shuffled back and forth in a hospital corridor. It was the aimless movement of one who had outlived his timeliness. A name was sounded. His name. He stopped and turned toward the sound, drawn instinctively toward that name. The name-caller was a nurse's aide pushing a cart with crushed ice and pitchers. The old man waited, leaning against the wall. When the aide arrived, a mumbled conversation followed. Disbelief, then joy, then determination registered on the old man's face. He had been conscripted to help distribute the pitchers of ice. Need had saved him. Mercy in a white uniform had just earned an honorary degree in psychology. The old man still shuffled, his hands trembled and efficiency ratings dropped drastically, but in his eyes one could tell that he had been touched by grace. The hospital aide feared that stamina could not stand the test. She pointed down the corridor and said, "We've got to go all the way to the end of the hall." Grace replied in a cracked voice, "Honey, I'd go to the end of the world with you." That is the substantive shadow of a *grace*ful religion.

Conclusion

God's Good News has *in*formed us, has become
treasure in earthen vessels. Phillips Brooks called
it "truth through personality" and labeled it
"preaching" which is fine as long as "personality"
is not limited to clergy. Robert Oppenheimer was
less professionally directive when he declared that
the best way to send an idea was to wrap it in a
person. Incarnation! *In*formed essence.

For more than two weeks I meandered through
Alexander Solzhenitsyn's novel, *August 1914*. It is
a profusion of characters, most with two or more
names apiece. Action moves back and forth

between the front lines of battle in Prussia and the beautiful steppe district, between Moscow and General Headquarters. It was hopeless. Yet, I had a reading investment of over four hundred pages. My Puritan background would not allow me to stop. Then in chapter 42 the author came out and said what he had been implying. Two young Russians had decided to join the army and were discussing their decision with a self-styled philosopher. The teacher said: ". . . while you may pray for the people and sacrifice everything for their good, you must never trample your own soul underfoot—for who knows when one of you may not be fated to catch an echo of the true, the secret order of the world?"[1]

History, continued the teacher, has its own "organic structure."

Echo chambers—that's the form; truth—that's the essence. God has spoken saving word; do we not hear the echo? Hear not a new word or a different word but the same word that was spoken. Church is an echo chamber in which that word reverberates.

Every analogy, just as every form, has its weakness. It cannot carry the freight without breaking down along the way. Soren Kierkegaard used another sounding image. The post horn, he

[1] Alexander Solzhenitsyn, *August 1914* (New York: Farrar, Straus & Giroux, 1972) p. 410.

111

wrote, best expressed the essence of life. From this instrument one could never be certain of producing the same note twice in succession nor could one be certain in advance what note would be sounded. The person who offers a post horn to a friend with the polite request that he use it has explained everything. Kierkegaard wrote:

> This is my symbol. As the ascetics of old placed a skull upon the table and by the contemplation of it directed their meditations, so shall the post-horn upon my table always remind me of what the significance of life really is. Hail to the post-horn![2]

This is as useful a way as any I know to say that essence cannot be indubitably formed, but it will be formed. Pablo Picasso knew what he was talking about when he said that art was a lie that convinced him of the truth.

Religion is a lie that convinces us of the truth. Within this form, these forms, faith happens. Our frustration, if we allow it, has to do with faith's essence: what we want others to have, we cannot give to them. We can offer forms only, create new forms, arrange forms to enable experience. We can prepare the way of the Lord and shout *Maranatha*—and wait.

[2]Kierkegaard, *Repetition* (New York: Harper & Brothers, 1964), pp. 80-81.